The POW! Anthology

An illustrated anthology of poets, singer-songwriters, musicians and performance artists of the world

— to celebrate, commemorate and consolidate
the first Poetry Olympics Weekend festival

GW00468317

New Departures
Issues 21–22

to Merry
Christmas 96
love from Eva

Published in 1996 by
New Departures, PO Box 9819, London W11 2GQ.

A catalogue record for this book is available from the British Library.
ISBN 0 902689 17 7

The POW! Anthology
Edited by Michael Horovitz & Inge Elsa Laird
Designed by Satpaul Bhamra
Layout by Maja Prausnitz

Contents

Introduction

This is a spontaneous bop collection rattled together over a
weekend in order to coincide with, celebrate, and extend the
impact of London's First Poetry Olympics Weekend – POW!

31 summers ago I was one of 17 poets from 9 countries who
filled the Royal Albert Hall to overflowing with a high-spirited
reading grandiosely entitled 'The First International Poetry
Incarnation'. Some highspots from that evening have continued
reaching many further auditors via Peter Whitehead's *cinema
verité* film of the occasion, *Wholly Communion*. For Philip
French of the New Statesman it was ". . . my St Crispin's
Day/Agincourt moment of the 1960s, the Public occasion of the
past ten years one would most have regretted missing."

Now that I'm twice the age I was then, it feels time to hand
on a baton to future generations, with another grand-scale
demonstration of the far-reaching (r)evolutions that have
liberated poets and poetries over these decades. In 1960 Adrian
Mitchell prefaced his first book of poems: "Most people ignore
most poetry, because most poetry ignores most people."
Since then, the universal restoration of the lyre to the lyric and
of the original, telling lyric to all forms of music, has virtually
reversed this.

So have the allied energies of adventursome publishers, from
Anvil Press Poetry and *New Departures*, to Bloodaxe Books and
Penguin Modern Poets – and of intermedic bandwagons like
Jazz Poetry SuperJam and Poetry Olympics – to help the living
arts overcome every barrier of race and creed, dialect and style,
age and youth, gender and politics.

The Poetry Olympics looks to consolidate more inroads than its
(un)sporting counterpart does at Healing the Nations, with a
genuinely popular body of voices in pursuit of musical and
literary brilliance. We hope the Olympics in Atlanta, Georgia
will refract this spiritual and imaginative communality.

This year's festival, culminating in the Royal Albert Hall's first
International Poetry, Music And Sunday Songfeast, includes four
of the poets from 1965: Christopher Logue, Adrian Mitchell, the

Michael Horovitz

Russian laureate Andrei Voznesensky and myself. But the 1996
Weekend is designed to display the magnificent flowering of
poetry and performance arts which has grown so continuously
since that heady 'missionary' gig, with special emphasis on
musical, female, and multi-racial developments.

This plenitudinous feast should help bring home to the larger
public just how communicatively the performing arts are now
bearing fruit across the planet; how the ever-strengthening input
of intermedic artistic talents, worldwide, reaffirms the original
Olympic spirit; and how much of the best new poetry, comedy,
folk, rock, pop music and jazz replenishes the global
commitment, passion, and continuity of the love generation.

My thanks to every contributor to this anthology and to the
three events on 5–7 July – the International Poetry and Music
Prelude at Poets' Corner, Westminster Abbey; the Children's
Poetry Party at The Tabernacle, Notting Hill; and the marathon
jamboree at Royal Albert Hall – A Hip Mass : The SuperJam.
And equally inexhaustable buckets of gratitude to the multitude
of friends who helped the festival, and this, its enduring
monument, to happen. There's no space or time to name and
thank each of you individually, but you surely know what you've
done to help. May you never live to regret it. From each
according to their ability – to each according to their need.

Hoping you will enjoy this book – in haste but sincerely,

Michael Horovitz

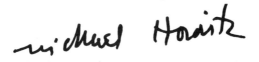

A Message from the Poet Laureate

It's so long now since those international Poetry frolics passed away, this is probably a good time to start something fresh.

... However rootedly-national in detail it may be, poetry is less and less the prisoner of its own language. It is beginning to represent, as an ambassador, something far greater than itself. Or perhaps it is only now being heard for what, among other things, it is – a universal language of understanding, coherent behind the many languages, in which we can all hope to meet. The idea of global unity is not new, but the absolute necessity of it has only just arrived, like a sudden radical alteration of the sun, and we shall have to adapt or disappear. If the various nations are ever to make a working synthesis of their fierce contradictions, the plan of it and the temper of it will be created in spirit before it can be formulated or accepted in political fact.

Ted Hughes

And it is in poetry that we can refresh our hope that such a unity is occupying people's imaginations everywhere, since poetry is the voice of spirit and imagination and all that is potential, as well as of the healing benevolence that used to be the privilege of the gods.

It is not enough to say this once. It has to be said afresh year after year, in as many places and different languages as possible. And the effort of poets them-selves to live up to their calling has to be renewed also, year after year ...

John Agard

Utterance

One humming bird morning
woman say to man
                    i feel so divine
                    i want to feel you wine
                        like a eel
                    between dis pum-pum of mine

such candour
made grass blush
every insect bristled

and hunger
crawled on all fours

                    seeking utterance

Accidentally Falling

Cheers
to the not
so distant
past They
always say
the first
sip is the
accidentally
falling in
lust period
Had we never
met each other
happened to fall
together entwined
I would not vintage
that bitter-sweet taste of
lips met over a glass of wine
experience ninesummersrolled
deliciously into our one green
bottle Caressed by the waves
we went the way of all lovers
when tipsy swaying to the hum of
summer bees our lust dried up
ran through fingers like sand
We noticed one-another's faults
your eyes took on that half-empty
half-hearted all is over look
You laughed when my jokes were
serious I cried when we were
bodily united mentally untied
tossing on a grey pebble beach
desperate scraping the barrel
making it up only to quarrel
making nothing but memories
drew the whole thing out until
it was out of control finished
sentimental dust I relive it
annually smiling vacant over
a bottle of wine now it's over
past just like the other nine

Patience Agbabi

essex dogs

A   down rememberance avenue
       dogs somersault through sprinklers on summer lawns
       and on the plains of cement
B   the english army grind their teeth
         in terminal pubs

       besty scores a hatrick
       he drinks ,he fights,he fucks   ———*everywhere*

C   6 a.m is awash in violet dulux
     andthe essex dogs are all loved up

Damon Albarn

This Is A Low

and into the sea goes pretty England and me
around the Bay of Biscay and back for tea
hit traffic on the Dogger Bank
up the Thames to find a taxi rank
sail on by with the tide and go asleep
and the radio says

this is a low
but it won't hurt you
when you are alone it will be there with you
finding ways to stay solo

on the Tyne, Forth and Cromity
there's a low in the high forties
and Saturday's locked away on the pier
not fast enough dear
on the Malin Head, Blackpool looks blue and red
and the Queen, she's gone round the bend
jumped off Land's End

this is a low
but it won't hurt you
when you are alone it will be there with you
finding ways to stay solo

Damon Albarn

Parklife

confidence is a preference for the habitual voyeur of what is
    known as (parklife)
and morning soup can be avoided if you take a route straight
    through what is known as (parklife)
John's got brewer's droop he gets intimidated by the dirty
    pigeons they love a bit of it (parklife)
who's that gut lord marching . . . you should cut down on your
    porklife mate . . . get some exercise

all the people
so many people
they all go hand in hand
hand in hand through their parklife

know what I mean
I get up when I want except on Wednesdays when I get rudely
    awakened by the dustmen (parklife)
I put my trousers on, have a cup of tea and I think about leaving
    the house (parklife)
I feed the pigeons I sometimes feed the sparrows too it gives me a
    sense of enormous well-being (parklife)
and then I'm happy for the rest of the day safe in the knowledge
    there will always be a bit of my heart devoted to it (parklife)

all the people
so many people
they all go hand in hand
hand in hand through their parklife

parklife (parklife)
parklife (parklife)

it's got nothing to do with vorsprung durch technik you know
and it's not about you joggers who go round and round and
    round

parklife (parklife)

all the people
so many people
they all go hand in hand
hand in hand through their parklife

Damon Albarn

girls and boys

street is like a jungle
so call the police
following the herd
down to greece
on holiday
love in the 90s
is paranoid
on sunny beaches
take your chances looking for

girls who are boys
who like boys to be girls
who do boys like they're girls
who do girls like they're boys
always should be someone you really love

avoiding all work
because there's none available
like battery thinkers
count their thoughts on 1 2 3 4 5 fingers
nothing is wasted
only reproduced
get nasty blisters
du bist sehr schön
but we haven't been introduced

girls who are boys
who like boys to be girls
who do boys like they're girls
who do girls like they're boys
always should be someone you really love

Damon Albarn

one chord seq.
Gm / C / F / E♭ (F#/F)

Ferondo's Wife in a Fit of Depression

Simon Armitage

described to the abbot
one day in confession

how her husband was more than just averagely jealous
and hated her meeting or speaking with fellers.

The abbot reflected that he could save her
in return for certain physical favours;

she agreed,
and next week

Ferondo was drugged with a measured proportion
of an ancient and powerful sleeping potion

then dragged away and locked in a shed,
and when he woke up he was told he was dead,

or more precisely that this prison cell
was that no-man's land between earth and hell.

A monk came by each evensong and with a rod he
thrashed the green-eyed monster from Ferondo's body.

Meanwhile, cavorting with the abbot every day
had left Ferondo's woman in the family way,

so the abbot, disguised as the Lord God Almighty
announced to Ferondo that things were alright, he

could rejoin his wife
and return to life,

and if he should alter his ways then maybe, and just maybe,
the good Lord would honour them both with a baby.

The abbot's esteem in the parish was doubled
for the way people felt he had counselled the couple,

and the family were blessed with a son and heir.
For her own part, the wife carried on her affair

with the abbot, to tempt her husband perhaps
to renege on his deal with the Lord, to lapse

if he dared.
But he was too scared.

Simon Armitage

On an Afternoon Train from Purley to Victoria, 1955

Hello, she said and startled me.
Nice day. Nice day I agreed.
I am a Quaker she said and Sunday
I was moved in silence
to speak a poem loudly
for racial brotherhood.

I was thoughtful, then said
what poem came on like that?
One the moment inspired she said.
I was again thoughtful.

Inexplicably I saw
empty city streets lit dimly
in a day's first hours.
Alongside in darkness
was my father's big banana field.

Where are you from? she said
Jamaica I said.
What part of Africa is Jamaica? she said.
Where Ireland is near Lapland I said.
Hard to see why you leave
such sunny country she said.
Snow falls elsewhere I said.
So sincere she was beautiful
as people sat down around us.

James Berry

Sujata Bhatt

Chutney

The diaspora women who thought Culture
meant being able to create
a perfect mango chutney in New Jersey
were scorned by the visiting scholar
from Bombay – who was also a woman
but unmarried and so different.
Sachi was her name, meaning "Truth".
And her greatest wish was to travel further north
to have a look
at Wallace Stevens' house. Once there

she circled the huge box-like wooden house
painted a dull white. It loomed.
It was far too awkward in the small yard.
She looked up
towards the trees, looked down at the road –
And her eyes
for once not analytical
became the eyes of the poorest Bombay woman
visiting a temple.

Valerie Bloom

Sun a-shine, rain a-fall

Sun a-shine an' rain a-fall,
The Devil an' him wife cyan 'gree at all,
The two o' them want one fish-head,
The Devil call him wife bonehead,
She hiss her teeth, call him cock-eye,
Greedy, worthless an' workshy,
While them busy callin' name,
The puss walk in, sey is a shame
To see a nice fish go to was'e,
Lef' with a big grin pon him face.

Rain a-fall

Rain a-fall, breeze a-blow,
All the washing deh a doah,
Nothing sharp like granny tongue
When breeze blow the wash-line dung.

Language

My tongue – forked like a snake's
but without deadly intentions:
just a bilingual hissing.

Description of the Hand

The fifth finger is an ornament.
The third one is symmetry's axle.
The thumb is meant to grab.
The fourth plays a lesser role.
The second is Adam's (and God's) forefinger.

trs: Brenda Walker and Nina Cassian

A Famous Woman

Lady Macbeth had a goal,
Lady Macbeth had a vision.
Preparing for an essential birth,
totally barren she remained.

If instead of her clear vision
she had merely had offspring,
who would ever have heard of her?

trs: William Jay Smith

Nina Cassian

Repetitio

A blade of grass
a curved blade of grass,
curved like an eyelash, a blade of grass,
a blade of grass piercing the earth,
sweetening its desert,
a blade of grass counting out my seasons,
one by one,
four by four,
waiting calmly for me to become
a blade of grass,
a blade of grass.

trs: Nina Cassian

Nina Cassian

Black Hair

Last night my kisses were banked in black hair
And in my bed, my lover, her hair was midnight black
And her mystery dwelled within her black hair
And her black hair framed a happy heart-shaped face

And heavy-hooded eyes inside her black hair
Shined at me from the depths of her hair of deepest black
While my fingers pushed and curled into her straight black hair
Pulling her black hair back from her happy heart-shaped face

To kiss her milk-white throat, a dark curtain of black hair
Smothered me, my lover with her beautiful black hair
The smell of it is heavy. It is charged with life
On my fingers the smell of her deep black hair

Full of all my whispered words, her black hair
And wet with tears and goodbyes, her hair of deepest black
All my tears cried against her milk-white throat
Hidden behind the curtain of her beautiful black hair

As deep as ink and black, black as the deepest sea
The smell of her black hair upon my pillow
Where her head and all its black hair did rest
Today she took a train to the West, to the West
Today she took a train to the West

Nick Cave

hire car

double park don't lock the door
push the pedals through the floor
give it loads and then some more
it's a hire car baby

grip the stick grind the gears
watch that distance disappear
never be yours in a thousand years
it's a hire car baby

hire car hire car
why would anybody buy a car
bang it prang it say ta ta
it's a hire car baby

bad behaviour on the street
save yourself a couple of sheets
collision waiver keeps it sweet
it's a hire car baby

drive the fucker anywhere
just like you don't care
put it down to wear and tear
it's a hire car baby

pray the person who hired it last
didn't drive it quite so fast
this dagenham dodgem doesn't last
it's a hire car baby

try not to kill yourself
or injure anybody else
don't forget to fasten your belts
it's a hire car baby

rent it
dent it
bang it
prang it
bump it

John Cooper Clarke

dump it
scorch it
torch it
crash and burn it
don't return it
lost deposit
let 'em earn it
who cares it's on
the firm it's
a hire car baby

TOM JONES
Back in town in a black Rollo Royce
the funky hunky housewives choice
in one fact he can rejoice
his trousers don't affect his voice

Haiku
to convey one's mood
in seventeen syllables
is very diffic

John Cooper Clarke

Art Lover

Sunday afternoon there's something special,
      it's just like another world
Jogging in the park is my excuse to look at all the little girls
I'm not a flasher in a raincoat, I'm not a dirty old man
I'm not gonna snatch you from your mother.
I'm an art lover.
Come to Daddy

Pretty little legs
I want to draw them like a Degas ballerina
Pure white skin, like porcelain.
She's a work of art, and I should know
I'm an art lover

Little girl, don't notice me, watching as she innocently plays
She can't see me staring at her because I'm always wearing shades
She feeds the ducks, looks at the flowers
I follow her around for hours and hours
I'd take her home, but that can never be
She's just a substitute for what's been taken from me

Sunday afternoon can't last forever, wish I could take you home
So come on, give us a smile
Before you vanish out of view
I've learned to appreciate you the way art lovers do
And I only want to look at you.

Ray Davies

Litany

The soundtrack then was a litany – *candlewick*
bedspread three piece suite display cabinet –
and stiff-haired wives balanced their red smiles,
passing the catalogue. *Pyrex.* A tiny ladder
ran up Mrs Barr's American Tan leg, sly
like a rumour. Language embarrassed them.

The terrible marriages crackled, cellophane
round polyester shirts, and then The Lounge
would seem to bristle with eyes, hard
as the bright stones in engagement rings,
and sharp hands poised over biscuits as a word
was spelled out. An embarrassing word, broken

to bits, which tensed the air like an accident.
This was the code I learnt at my mother's knee, pretending
to read, where no one had cancer, or sex, or debts,
and certainly not leukaemia, which no one could spell.
The year a mass grave of wasps bobbed in a jam-jar;
a butterfly stammered itself in my curious hands.

A boy in the playground, I said, *told me*
to fuck off; and a thrilled malicious pause
salted my tongue like an imminent storm. Then
uproar. *I'm sorry, Mrs Barr, Mrs Hunt, Mrs Emery,*
sorry Mrs Raine. Yes, I can summon their names.
My mother's mute shame. The taste of soap.

Carol Ann Duffy

Paul Durcan

Raymond of the Rooftops

The morning after the night
The roof flew off the house
And our sleeping children narrowly missed
Being decapitated by falling slates,
I asked my husband if he would
Help me put back the roof:
But no – he was too busy at his work
Writing for a women's magazine in London
An Irish fairy tale called *Raymond of the Rooftops*.
Will you have a heart, woman – he bellowed –
Can't you see I am up to my eyes and ears in work,
Breaking my neck to finish *Raymond of the Rooftops*,
Fighting against time to finish *Raymond of the Rooftops*,
Putting everything I have got into *Raymond of the Rooftops*?

Isn't it well for him? *Everything he has got!*

All I wanted him to do was to stand
For an hour, maybe two hours, three at the most,
At the bottom of the stepladder
And hand me up slates while I slated the roof:
But no – once again I was proving to be the insensitive,
Thoughtless, feckless even, wife of the artist.
There was I up to my fat, raw knees in rainwater
Worrying him about the hole in our roof
While he was up to his neck in *Raymond of the Rooftops*.
Will you have a heart, woman – he bellowed –
Can't you see I am up to my eyes and ears in work,
Breaking my neck to finish *Raymond of the Rooftops*,
Fighting against time to finish *Raymond of the Rooftops*,
Putting everything I have got into *Raymond of the Rooftops*?

Isn't it well for him?
      Everything he has got!

The Mistake

With the mistake your life goes in reverse.
Now you can see exactly what you did
Wrong yesterday and wrong the day before
And each mistake leads back to something worse

And every nuance of your hypocrisy
Towards yourself, and every excuse
Stands solidly on the perspective lines
And there is perfect visibility.

What an enlightenment. The Colonnade
Rolls past on either side. You needn't move.
The statues of your errors brush your sleeve.
You watch the tale turn back – and you're dismayed.

And this dismay at this, this big mistake
Is made worse by the sight of all those who
Knew all along where these mistakes would lead –
Those frozen friends who watched the crisis break.

Why didn't they *say*? Oh, but they did indeed –
Said with a murmur when the time was wrong
Or by a mild refusal to assent
Or told you plainly but you would not heed.

Yes, you can hear them now. It hurts. It's worse
Than any sneer from any enemy.
Take this dismay. Lay claim to this mistake.
Look straight along the lines of this reverse.

James Fenton

Justine Frischmann

line up

drivel head wears her glad rags
she's got her keysmoneyandfags
  i know that her mind is made up
to get rocked

drivel head needs a new man
as only a drivel head can
he's a hormonal nightmare
so beware

  drivel head knows all the stars
  loves to suck their shining guitars
  they've all been right up her stairs
do you care?

drivel head loves the new band
  knows them like the back of her hand
you can't see the wood for the trees
  on your knees

Menu Poem

mice in cheese sauce
eggshells with shoe polish and rice
nice clean socks in a box of yoghurt and dog hairs
umbrellas full of chips
followed by chocolate ice cream with worms

Donkey Dentist Poem

Please

Open

Ee-aw

Mouth

Parental Pressure Poem

Parents

Only

Expect

Miracles.

John Hegley

Red Poem

Danger!
Don't tip that strawberry jam
into the post box.
Stop! Stop! If the post office van
turns up now,
you'll be so embarrassed,
Dad.

Miroslav Holub

Great Ancestors

At night
their silhouettes are outlined
against the empty sky
like a squadron of Trojan horses.
Their whispers rise from wells
of apparently living water.

But when day breaks
the way an egg cracks
and full-grown men with truncheons are born,
and mothers bleed profoundly,

they turn into butterflies
with cabbage leaves for wings,
to jelly condensed from fog
in fading, babyish outlines,

their barely discernible hands
shake,

they forget to breathe,
and are afraid to speak a single
intelligible word.

Anyway,
we've picked up more genes from viruses
than from them.

They have no strength.
And we must be the strength of those
who have no strength.

trs: David Young and Dana Hàbovà

A Song for Frances

I hear you call my head a bin
Where children dip their buckets in

As I float and tinkle in the sky
The sun at your mermaid tail doth fly

Earth sings through you from where oceans flow
Nourishing forests aeons below

Where jellyfish squish at the plashing barrel
Of starfood – where no man picks a quarrel

You ward off the flies with a wand of fresh fernlets
You come softly to mind in a clearing of dreams

Whilst the moon falls asleep as the cock greets the sun
We walk air, tread water
                              – bird and fish as one.

Michael Horovitz

Sisyphan

Michael Horovitz

I dreamed I'd written down
the dream
straight off
in its pure dream mode
untranslatable to man

and so was safe
from any scheme
to amplify, thus cloud
what it might mean

to no avail:

for when I woke
at first serene
but then, alas – the dream
was nowhere to be seen

no trace
beyond my certainty
that in it I'd conceived
the poem I was born for

lost now, indifferent
as death to breath
to how
each night, each day

words fail

My Life with Dylan Thomas

I have loved Dylan Thomas since I was seventeen. Well, he's
Welsh, he's funny, he's passionate and he's a poet – what more
could a girl want? Although he died in a hospital in New York in
1953, he is alive and singing with 'hwyl' in his extraordinary
poems and stories.

I had a wonderful year with Dylan last year at the National
Theatre. I was part of an all-Welsh cast in a production of *Under
Milk Wood* at the Olivier Theatre. Certainly part of the terror
and excitement of each performance was being suspended fifty
feet above the stage in a double bed for the first fifteen minutes
of the play, before being flown in and lowered onto the stage to
berate my two poor dead husbands, either side of me in bed –
Mr Ogmore and Mr Pritchard.

Dylan as a boy fantasised about flying above his home in Wales.
Swooping self-propelled, above streets and lanes and woods,
observing life from his own aerial viewpoint. Roger Michell, the
director, and the designer Bill Dudley (English, but definitely our
soul brother in Wales) brilliantly used this lifelong obsession of
Dylan's by flying actors and beds and all sorts of things,
magically and dreamily, above the sleeping village of Llareggub,
on the stage below.

Dylan and *Under Milk Wood* have been flying in and out of my
life since I started in the theatre. Lily Smalls won me the prize of
a six-month contract with the BBC Drama Repertory Company
from Drama School. Then, as part of an audition for the Royal
Shakespeare company, she brought me luck again. To tell the
truth, I can chart my inevitable ageing process by my parts in
Under Milk Wood over the years. I played Mae Rose Cottage
"Seventeen and never been sweet in the grass ho ho" on BBC TV
in the early Sixties, with Donald Houston as a brilliant and
lyrical 1st Voice. Then, in a stage production at Leicester, I played
Polly Garter and Rosie Probert – still sexy, but a bit more
mature. In a quadraphonic radio production directed by
Douglas Cleverdon (who directed the original radio production),
I played Polly Garter again, with Donald Houston as 1st Voice
and many splendid Welsh actors who had been in the very first
broadcast of *Under Milk Wood*.

Nerys Hughes

In a production at the Duke of York's Theatre, in aid of a memorial plaque for Dylan in Poets' Corner at Westminster Abbey, I played Polly Garter for the third time. Richard Burton as 1st Voice led a hugely talented Welsh cast, and brought Elizabeth Taylor (his then wife) onto the stage – to an ecstatic reception from the audience!

George Martin made a wonderfully musical CD, with a very starry Welsh cast – including Tom Jones, Harry Secombe, Sian Phillips, Mary Hopkin and Ruth Madoc. Tony Hopkins played 1st Voice and Jonathan Pryce was 2nd Voice. Now I'm well into middle age, playing Mrs Ogmore Pritchard and Mrs Day Bread One.

I've only got one part left to play in my old age – Mary Ann the Sailors, who is eighty!

Nerys Hughes

Under Milk Wood is a day in the life of a little village in Wales called Llareggub. It starts on a "spring, moonless night" and we hear the dreams and fears of the sleeping villagers. It is a sexually charged, irreverent, exuberant, wonderfully wordy play – and tonight at Albert Hall I'm at it again, with the legendary Stan Tracey this time – what *Hwyl*!

Sugar-coated Pill

A clever adversary
does not advertise his intentions.
He will come with a big smile
to show his love; and slogans
that even you would hesitate to shout.
Freedom, Peace and Equality
will never be far from his lips
and he will offer every help
to keep you where you are.
A split soul, a lost language
the poison of gifts
the symptoms of slow penetration.
Fantasies on the screen,
arguments that are "self evident"
And you feel a romantic fool
for trying to change the world.
"Be my wife, my child
and all shall be well."
Flowers, chocolates, perfumes, gadgets
his subtle armaments; what else
could you ask for
being hopelessly divided
friendless, faceless, full of fears.
And while you man the barricades
in battledress keeping an eye out for
intruders,
He surprises you with an embrace.
You have been disarmed!

Mahmood Jamal

Dance of the Cherry Blossom

Both of us are getting worse
Neither knows who had it first

He thinks I gave it to him
I think he gave it to me

Nights chasing clues where
One memory runs into another like dye.

Both of us are getting worse
I know I'm wasting precious time

But who did he meet between
May 87 and March 89.

I feel his breath on my back
A slow climb into himself then out.

In the morning it all seems different
Neither knows who had it first

We eat breakfast together – newspapers
And silence except for the slow slurp of tea

This companionship is better than anything
He thinks I gave it to him.

By lunchtime we're fighting over some petty thing
He tells me I've lost my sense of humour

I tell him I'm not Glaswegian
You all think death is a joke

It's not funny. I'm dying for fuck's sake
I think he gave it to me.

Just think he says it's every couple's dream
I won't have to wait for you up there

Jackie Kay

I'll have you night after night – your glorious legs
Your strong hard belly, your kissable cheeks

I cry when he says things like that
My shoulders cave in, my breathing trapped

Do you think you have a corner on dying
You self-pitying wretch, pathetic queen.

He pushes me; we roll on the floor like whirlwind;
When we are done in, our lips find each other

We touch soft as breeze, caress the small parts
Rocking back and forth, his arms become mine

There's nothing outside but the noise of the wind
The cherry blossoms dance through the night.

Jackie Kay

Bridge

and in the dark to lean across
like a bridge over a river on whose bed
stones are untroubled by what passes
overhead
and kiss the sleep in your body
with I love you I love you
like currents through my head
that is closer to deep water now
than at any time of the day

Ambulance

Shrieking on its mercy mission,
The white hysterical bully
Blows all things out of its way,
Cutting through the slack city
Like a knife through flesh.
People respect potential saviours
And immediately step aside,
Watching it pitch and scream ahead,
Ignoring the lights, breaking the rules,
Lurching on the crazy line
Between the living and the dead.

The Scarf

It strayed about her head and neck like a
Rumour of something she had never done
Because, the moment ripe, she had no mind to
Yet might have done often, had she chosen.
Where in God's name, I wondered, does it begin
And where on earth may I imagine its end?
Indolent headlands smiled at me, labyrinthine
Rivers flowing into each other wound
And wound about her like desires to praise
Every movement that her body made.
As she moved, so did headlands, rivers too,
Shifting with her as the winter sun laid
Emphasis on colours rumoured in its rays,
Grey-flecked lines of white, delirium of blue.

Brendan Kennelly

Brendan Kennelly

Wings

The words have been said.
He towers above her, she pretends he's not there,
She concentrates on washing a heart of lettuce,
Wet leaves glitter in her fingers.
He folds his hand like wings about her black hair
And kisses her head.

A Short Story

"For *Hunger*, a short story by James Stephens,
I am bid eleven pounds!"
The auctioneer
With fat red-faced finality
Brings his hammer down.
I think how Stephens
Suffering, remote,
Trudged Dublin streets,
Brooding on the singers and the wise,
Wolves of hunger prowling in his heart,
Sorrow in his eyes.

D'Accord Baby

All week Bill had been looking forward to this moment. He was about to fuck the daughter of the man who had fucked his wife. Lying in her bed, he could hear Celestine humming in the bathroom as she prepared for him.

It had been a long time since he'd been in a room so cold, with no heating. After a while he ventured his arms over the covers, tore open a condom and lay the rubber on the cardboard box which served as a bedside table. He was about to prepare another, but didn't want to appear over-optimistic. One would achieve his objective. He would clear out then. Already there had been too many delays. The waltz, for instance, though it made him giggle. Nevertheless he had told his Madelaine, his pregnant wife, that he would be back by midnight. What could Celestine be doing in there? There wasn't even a shower; and the wind cut viciously through the broken window.

His wife had met Celestine's father, Vincent Ertel, the French ex-Maoist intellectual, in Paris. He had certainly impressed her. She had talked about him continually, which was bad enough, and then rarely mentioned him, which, as he understood now, was worse.

Madelaine worked on a late-night TV discussion programme. For two years she had been eager to profile Vincent's progresss from revolutionary to Catholic reactionary. It was, she liked to inform Bill – using a phrase that stayed in his mind – indicative of the age. Several times she went to see Vincent in Paris; then she was invited to his country place near Auxerre. Finally she brought him to London to record the interview. When it was done, to celebrate, she took him to Le Caprice for champagne, fishcakes and chips.

That night Bill had put aside the script he was directing and gone to bed early with a ruler, pencil and *The Brothers Karamazov*. Around the time that Madelaine was becoming particularly enthusiastic about Vincent, Bill had made up his mind not only to study the great books – the most dense and intransigent, the ones from which he'd always flinched – but to underline them, and even to memorise certain passages. The effort to concentrate was a torment, as his mind flew about. Yet most nights – even during the period when Madelaine was preparing for her encounter with Vincent – he kept his light on long after she had put hers out. Determined to swallow the thickest pills of understanding, he would lie there muttering phrases he wanted to retain. One of his favourites was Emerson's, "We but half express ourselves, and are ashamed of that divine idea which each of us represents."

One night Madelaine opened her eyes and with a quizzical look said, "Can't you be easier on yourself?"

Why? He wouldn't give up. He had read biology at university. Surely he couldn't be such a fool as to find these books beyond him? His need for knowledge, wisdom, nourishment was more than his need for sleep. How could a man have come to the middle of his life with barely a clue about who he was or where he might go? The heavy volumes represented the highest, surely, that man's thought had flown; they had to include guidance.

The close, leisurely contemplation afforded him some satisfaction – usually because the books started him thinking about other things. It was the part of the day he preferred. He slept well, usually. But at four, on the long night of the fishcakes, he awoke and felt for Madelaine across the bed. She wasn't there. Shivering, he walked through the house until dawn, imagining she'd crashed the car. After an hour he remembered she hadn't taken it. Maybe she and Vincent had gone on to a late-night place. She had never done anything like this before.

He could neither sleep nor go to work. He decided to sit at the kitchen table until she returned, whenever it was. He was drinking brandy, and normally he never drank before eight in the evening. If anyone offered him a drink before this time, he claimed it was like saying goodbye to the whole day. In the mid-'80s he'd gone to the gym in the early evening. For some days, though, goodbye was surely the most suitable word.

It was late afternoon before his wife returned wearing the clothes she'd gone out in, looking dishevelled and uncertain. She couldn't meet his eye. He asked her what she'd been doing. She said, "What d'you think?" and went into the shower.

He had considered several options, including punching her. But he fled the house and made it to a pub. For the first time since he'd been a student he sat alone with nothing to do. He was expected nowhere. He had no newspaper with him, and he liked papers; he could swallow the most banal and incredible thing

Hanif Kureishi

provided it was on newsprint. He watched the passing faces and thought how pitiless the world was if you didn't have a safe place in it.

He made himself consider how unrewarding it was to constrain people. Infidelities would occur in most relationships. These days every man and woman was a cuckold. And why not, when marriage was insufficient to satisfy the most human need? Madelaine had needed something and she had taken it. How bold and stylish. How petty to blame someone for pursuing any kind of love!

He was humiliated. The feeling increased over the weeks in a strange way. At work or waiting for the tube, or having dinner with Madelaine – who had gained, he could see, a bustling dismissive intensity of will or concentration – he found himself becoming angry with Vincent. For days on end he couldn't, really, think of anything else, as if the man were inhabiting him.

As he walked around Soho, where he worked, Bill entertained himself by thinking of how someone might get even with a type like Vincent, were he so inclined. The possibility was quite remote but this didn't prevent him imagining stories from which he emerged with some satisfaction, if not credit. What incentive, distraction, energy and interest Vincent provided him with! This was almost the only creative work he got to do now.

A few days later he was presented with Celestine, sitting with a man in a newly opened cafe, drinking cappuccino. Life was giving him a chance. It was awful. He stood in the doorway pretending to look for someone and thought whether he should take it.

Vincent's eldest daughter lived in London. She wanted to be an actress and Bill had auditioned her for a commercial a couple of years ago, and he knew she'd obtained a small part in a film directed by an acquaintance of his. On this basis he crossed the cafe, introduced himself, made the pleasantest conversation he could, and was invited to sit down. The man turned out to be a gay friend of hers. They all chatted. After some timorous vacillation Bill asked Celestine in a cool tone whether she'd have a drink with him in a couple of hours.

He didn't go home then but walked about. When he was tired he sat in a pub with the first volume of *Remembrance of Things Past*. He had decided that if he could read to the end of the whole book he would deserve a great deal of praise. He did a little underlining, which since school he had considered a sign of seriousness, but his mind wandered even more than usual, until it was time to meet her.

To his pleasure Bill saw that men glanced at Celestine when they could; others openly stared. When she fetched a drink, they turned to examine her legs. This would not have happened with Madelaine; only Vincent Ertel had taken an interest in her. Later, as he and Celestine strolled up the street looking for cabs, she agreed that he would come to her place at the end of the week.

It was a triumphant few days of gratification anticipated. He would do more of this. He had obviously been missing out on life's meaner pleasures. As Madelaine walked about the flat, dressing, cooking, reading, searching for her glasses, he could enjoy despising her. He informed his two closest friends that the pleasures of revenge were considerable. He liked saying that the French were used to being occupied. Now his pals were waiting to hear of his coup.

Celestine flung the keys, wrapped in a tea-towel, out of the window. It was a hard climb; her flat was at the top of a five-storey run-down building in West London, an area of itinerants, bed-sits and students. Coming into the living room, he saw it had a view across a square. Wind and rain was sweeping into the cracked windows stuffed with newspaper. The walls were yellow, the carpet brown and stained. The gas fire, which had several pairs of jeans suspended in front of it on a clothes horse, gave off an odour and heated parts of the room while leaving others cold.

She persuaded him to remove his overcoat but not his scarf. Then she took him into the tiny kitchen with bare floor-boards where, between an old sink and the boiler, there was hardly room for the two of them.

"I will be having us some dinner." She pointed to two shopping bags. "Do you like troot?"

"Sorry?"

It was trout. There were potatoes and green beans. After, they would have apple strudel with cream. She had been to the shops and gone to some trouble. It would take ages to prepare. He hadn't anticipate this. He left her there, saying he would fetch drink.

Hanif Kureishi

In the rain he went to the off-licence and was paying for the wine when he noticed through the window that a taxi had stopped at traffic lights. He ran out of the shop to hail the cab, but as he opened the door couldn't go through with it. He collected the wine and carried it back.

He waited in her living room, pacing and drinking. She didn't have a TV. Wintry noises battered the window. Her place reminded him of rooms he'd shared as a student. He was about to say to himself, thank God I'll never have to live like this again, when it occurred to him that if he left Madelaine, he might, for a time, end up in some unfamiliar place, with stained, old, broken fittings. How fastidious he'd become! How had it happened! What other changes had there been, whilst he was looking in the other direction?

He noticed a curled photograph tacked to the wall which looked as though it had been taken at the end of the '60s. Bill concluded it was the hopeful radical who'd fucked his wife. He had been a handsome man, and with his pipe in his hand, hair below his ears and open-necked shirt, he had an engaging look of self-belief and raffish pleasure. Bill recalled the slogans that decorated Paris, "Everything is Possible" "Take Your Desires for Realities" "It is Forbidden to Forbid." He'd once used them in a TV commercial. What optimism that generation had had! With his life given over to literature, ideas, conversation, writing and political commitment, ol' Vincent must have had quite a nice time. He couldn't have been working constantly, like Bill and his friends.

The food was good. Bill leaned across the table to kiss Celestine. His lips brushed her cheek. She turned her head and looked out across the dark square to the lights beyond, as if trying to locate something.

He talked about the film industry and what the actors, directors and producers of the movies were really like. Not that he knew them personally, but they were gossiped about by other actors and technicians. She asked questions and laughed easily.

Things should have been moving along. He had to get up at 5.30 to direct a commercial for a bank. He was becoming known for such well-paid but journeyman work. Now that Madelaine was pregnant he would have to do more of it. It would be a struggle to find time for the screenwriting he wanted to do. It was dawning on him that if he were to do anything worthwhile at his age, he had to be serious in a new way. And yet when he considered his ambitions, which he no longer mentioned to anyone – to travel overland to Indonesia while reading Proust . . . and other, more "internal" things – he felt a surge of shame, as if it was immature and obscene to harbour such hopes, as if, in some ways, it was already too late.

He shuffled his chair around the table until he and Celestine were sitting side by side. He attempted another kiss.

She stood up and offered him her hands. "Shall we dance?"

He looked at her in surprise. "Dance?"

"It will 'ot you up. Don't you . . . dance?"

"Not really."

"Why?"

"Why? We always danced like that." He shut his eyes and nodded his head as if attempting to bang in a nail with his forehead.

She kicked off her shoes.

"We danced like this. I'll illustrate you." She looked at him. "Take it off."

"What?"

"This stupid thing."

She pulled off his scarf. She shoved the chairs against the wall and put on a Chopin waltz, took his hand and placed her other hand in his back. He looked down at her dancing feet even as he trod on them, but she didn't object. Gently but firmly she turned and turned him across the room, until he was dizzy, her hair tickling his face. Whenever he glanced up she was looking into his eyes. Each time they crossed the room, she trotted back, pulling him, never unamused. She seemed determined that he should learn, certain that this would benefit him.

"You require some practice," she said at last. He fell back into his chair blowing and laughing. "But after a week, who knows, we could be having you work as a gigolo!"

It was midnight. Celestine came naked out of the bathroom smoking a cigarette. She got into bed and lay beside him. He thought of a time in New York when the company sent a white limousine to the airport. Drinking whisky and watching TV as the limo passed over the Hudson towards Manhattan, he wanted nothing more than for his friends to see him.

She was on him vigorously and the earth was moving; either that, or the two single beds, on the juncture of which he was lying, were separating. He stuck out his arms to secure them, but with each lurch his head was being forced down into the fissure. He felt as if his ears were going to be torn off. The two of them were about to crash through onto the floor.

He rolled her over onto one bed. They he sat up and showed her what would have happened. She started to laugh, she couldn't stop.

The gas meter ticked; she was dozing. He had never lain beside a lovelier face. He thought of what Madelaine might have sought that night with Celestine's father. Affection, attention, serious talk, honesty, distraction. Did he give her that now? Could they give it to one another, and with a kid on the way?

Celestine was nudging him and trying to say something in his ear.

"You want what?" he said. Then, "Surely . . . no . . . no."

"Bill, yes."

He liked to think he was willing to try anything. A black eye would certainly send a convincing message to her father. She smiled when he raised his hand.

"I deserve to be hurt."

"No-one deserves that."

"But you see . . . I do."

That night, in the freezing room, he praised her beauty and her intelligence; he did everything she asked, for as long as she wanted – he had never kissed anyone for so long – until he forgot where he was, or who they both were, until there was nothing they wanted, and there was only the most satisfactory peace.

He got up and dressed. He was shivering. He wanted to wash, he smelled of her, but he wasn't prepared for a cold bath.

"Why are you leaving?" She leaped up and held him. "Stay, stay, I haven't finished with you yet."

He put on his coat and went into the living room. Without

Hanif Kureishi

looking back he hurried out and down the stairs. He pulled the front door, anticipating the fresh damp night air. But the door held. He had forgotten; the door was locked. He stood there.

Upstairs she was wrapped in a fur coat, looking out of the window.

"The key," he said.

"Old man," she said, laughing. "You are."

She accompanied him barefoot down the stairs. While she unlocked the door, he mumbled, "Will you tell your father I saw you?"

"But why?"

He touched her face. She drew back. "You should put something on that," he said. "I met him once. He knows my wife."

"I rarely see him now," she said.

She was holding out her arms. They danced a few steps across the hall. He was better at it now. He went out into the street. Several cabs passed him but he didn't hail them. He kept walking. There was comfort in the rain. He put his head back and looked up into the sky. He had some impression that happiness was beyond him and everything was coming down, and that nothing could be grasped but only lived.

Inge Elsa Laird

what little I have
I'll carry with me

what little I have
I carry on my shoulders

what little I have
is with me wherever I go

what little I have
is becoming unbearable

what little I have
runs through my fingers

what little I have
drifts quietly towards
                    the open window.

Time

Boiling eggs   takes
5 minutes
cutting bread   takes less
putting butter and
salt on the table
takes no time at all
the coffee is ready
it is time
to sit
and as we listen to the news
it becomes quite clear
we have no time   at all.

Fran Landesman

I Quite Like Men

I quite like men. They're rather sweet
I like to give them things to eat
They have nice hands and charming necks
And some of them are good at sex

My sympathies are feminist
But I am glad that men exist
Although they can be perfect swine
They're nice with candlelight and wine

They warm me up when I feel cold
And some of them have hearts of gold
They irritate me now and then
But on the whole
I quite like men

The Telegraph Baby (1916)

And now I remember the tall hussar
who gave me the halo of telegraph wire
which I wound round my body at the age of six.
Since then my hearing's been strangely acute,
for I watched as the workmen erected a line
of identical crosses all the way down
to the river that kept on discussing itself
out through the village, on to somewhere's sea . . .
He was huge in his dolman and when he saw

my delight at the splitting and hewing of wood
he called me closer to his brilliant braid;
then the world dipped and I could see the way
that men were cradled in the criss-cross tree,
hammering nonsense, till they left one man
like a Christ on the wire there, hanging alone
but listening to something that no one else heard.
My heart beat in dashes back down on the ground
and I knew that I'd learn how to understand

the metal's dispatches. Now, since the war
I've crossed high passes to talk in Morse
to other receivers, leading horses piled high
with the weight of talking, till I found my way
here to the trenches, to the news of troops,
disasters and weather, where now I'm stretched out,
nerves copper and all my circuits aware
they're transmitting a man on a wheel of barbed wire,
nothing but message, still tapping out fire.

Gwyneth Lewis

'Winter has flourished and gone'

Winter has flourished and gone
　　Drinking the last black frost.
The seeds clamber into the sun
　　and risen between our toes
Have parted the air and the earth.

　The light is with us.　Shall we cross?
　I hear the deepening river flow
Beneath us both who go to cast
　　our innocence away in love.

　　　Christopher Logue

Christopher Logue

The Man in the Moon

On the edge of the jumping-off place I stood
Below me, the lake
Beyond that, the dark wood
And above, a night-sky that roared.

I picked a space between two stars
Held out my arms and soared.

*   *   *

The journey lasted not half a minute
There is a moon reflected in the lake
You will find me in it.

Roger McGough

Uncle Sean

If they held Olympic Contests
for brick-throwing
Uncle Sean would win them all
at all.

But they don't.
So he carries hods for Wimpeys
and dreams of glories
that might have been.

Uncle Sean lives in Coventry
a stone's throw away
from the Albert Hall
at all.

Roger McGough

Roger McGough

Adrian Mitchell

A Puppy Called Puberty

It was like keeping a puppy in your underpants
A secret puppy you weren't allowed to show to anyone
Not even your best friend or your worst enemy

You wanted to pat him stroke him cuddle him
All the time but you weren't supposed to touch him

He only slept for five minutes at a time
Then he'd suddenly perk up his head
In the middle of school medical inspection
And always on bus rides
So you had to climb down from the upper deck
All bent double to smuggle the puppy off the bus
Without the buxom conductress spotting
Your wicked and ticketless stowaway.

Jumping up, wet-nosed, eagerly wagging –
He only stopped being a nuisance
When you were alone together
Pretending to be doing your homework
But really gazing at each other
Through hot and hazy daydreams

Of those beautiful schoolgirls on the bus
With kittens bouncing in their sweaters.

All Is Loneliness

Louis Hardin

Moondog

From Hardin's poetry collection 'Milleniad'

Moondog

I find the greatest freedom in the stricture of a form
that paradoxes abnormality within a norm.

The Sword of Damocles is hanging over all of us.
In view of that what subject can we sensibly discuss.

My credo may be this, that ere my dirth of days is passed,
I'll strive to live each one as if it were my first and last.

You pity me in exile? Well, then pity if you must,
but live – before your dear identity is lost in dust.

Carnivores who lived on Herbivores who lived on plants,
were all consumed by Omnivores who walked around in pants.

He who didn't know who didn't know he didn't know,
became the he who didn't know who knew he didn't know,
 and he became the he who knew who didn't know he knew,
who finally became the he who knew who knew he knew.

A glance, a smile, a chance hallo and then – a fond embrace.
The years roll back before my eyes to scenes I can't erase.

We grope with eyes wide open t'ward the darkness of futurity,
with faith in outermost instead of innermost security.

The trombone and the sackbut stare each other down in shame.
One sees what he had been, the other sees what he became.

The Whole declared, "You'll never know the sum of all My parts,
so stop your foolish figuring, and mend your broken hearts."

Proof that God exists is in the overtones from one
to nine, besides revealing how the Universe is run.

What I say of science here, I say without condition,
that science is the latest and the greatest superstition.

The Leaning Tower leaned a little farther south and said,
"I wouldn't be so famous if I had a level head."

A snow-flake landed on my hand and said, as if in fear,
"I must be on my way, before I turn into a tear."

Having healthy-wealthy possibility amounts
to nothing, if you do not know that every minute counts.

Moondog

Sugar Cane

Grace Nichols

1
There is something
about sugar cane

he isn't what
he seem –

indifferent hard
. and sheathed in blades

his waving arms
is a sign for help

his skin thick
only to protect
the juice inside
himself

2
His colour
is the aura
of jaundice
when he ripe

he shiver
like ague
when it rain

he suffer
from bellywork
burning fever
and delirium

just before
the hurricane
strike
smashing him to pieces

3
Growing up
is an art

he don't have
any control of

it is us
who groom and
weed him

who stick him
in the earth
in the first place

and when he
growing tall

with the help
of the sun
and rain

we feel the
need to strangle
the life

out of him

But either way he can't survive

Grace Nichols

4
Slowly
pain-
fully
sugar
cane
pushes
his
knotted
joints
upwards
from
the
earth
slowly
pain-
fully
he
comes
to learn
the
truth
about
himself
the
crimes
committed
in
his
name

5
He cast his shadow
to the earth

the wind is
his only mistress

I hear them
moving
in rustling tones

she shakes
his hard reserve

smoothing
stroking
caressing
all his length
shamelessly

I crouch
below them
quietly

Ben Okri

On a Picture of a South African Street

Our spirits grow weirder
Every night
Vengeance drags its long
And weary Shadow.

New vision could rise
From nightmare
Love and agony can light
The future.

On the farthest side of rainbow
Terror
We shall excavate the howling
Pot of human
Misery.

Virgil in Brindisi

He drifted into harbour
Lying in state
When the wine-drenched sea
Was clear as slate;

He dreamt of his great poem
Restless in him unfinished
And wept that twelve years
Beyond death were needed
For its perfection to be undiminished.

The great Emperor vertical
On another ship
Against a changing imperial sky
Could never have guessed
That in his poet's unrest
An eternal world would soar high.

"FULL FATHOME FIVE." Set by Robert Johnson, probably for the revival of *The Tempest* in 1613. *Source:* John Wilson, *Cheerfull Ayres* (1660).

Kazuko Shiraishi

Woodpecker

a woodpecker shows up, industriously
opening up a hole in a wooden house
a man flies out and threatens it

for 8 years the man
built a house
for his wife and 2 sons
then
before the woodpecker opened a hole
an invisible woodpecker arrived
and opened a hole in the man's wife

from there the wife
flew out somewhere
never to return again

a woodpecker shows up, industriously
pecking at a man's wooden house

Yellow Lake

you can catch fish there   delicious fish
and put them on your table
but the lake is yellow   hiding its depth
the Indians living by the lake
also hide their depth
maybe fish live in their eyes
or delicious spirits sing   boiling with hatred
the depths of their eyes are dark   no one can see
something lives   by the yellow lake
not showing its shape on the table

trs: John Solt

This little planet begins to
    have a headache
Since humans occupied it and
    took it out of God's hand
Green blood dries, earth's veins
    wither
The Whale gets harpooned before
    he sends singing Telepathy of Love
Big jet-flies circle the planet's
    head and turn the occident
    into a skull
Planet breaks its neck all thru
    21st century
Meanwhile killers get high on
    the God of Science
    & cheer the big Arms race on
Kicking the globe in the head and
    puncturing its skin
Earth looks like it won't recover,
    too many humans busy watching TV
And no one says anything about saving
    the planet
Will anyone witness our little
    Noah's Ark planet drown
    in the Universe?
Only if they're able to dig up a
    Time Capsule named the Future

trs: Allen Ginsberg

Kazuko Shiraishi

Natalia

Weaver of words
who lives alone
in fear & sorrow
Where is the word
that sets you free
perhaps tomorrow?
Where is the earth
where is the sky
where is the light you long for?
What hope have you
where you are now
Natalia Gorbanevskaya?

Inside the Ward
naked & cruel
where life is stolen
From those who try
to stay alive and still be human
Where are the friends
where are the men
who among them can defend you?
Where is the child
you never see
Natalia Gorbanevskaya?

What is there left
behind the door
that never opens?
Are you insane
as They say you are
or just forsaken?
Are you still there
do you still care
or are you lost forever?
I know this song
some day you'll hear
Natalia Gorbanevskaya!
Natalia Gorbanevskaya!

*Natalia was written for Natalia
Gorbanevskaya, a protegée of Alhmatova,
who was incarcerated in a 'psychiatric
ward' for being a dissident. Her letters
and poems were smuggled out of jail,
translated and published here; I read them,
was very moved and wrote the song.
As a result Amnesty took up her case and
campaigned for her, and she was chucked
out of Russia. She has been living in Paris
since the '70s. Joan Baez also recorded
the song and sang it all over the world.*

Shusha

Refugee

They said to him: "Why do you care?
What is it to you what happens where?
The world has always been the same –
Let the Devil dare!"

"It's foolish taking it to heart
When someone's jailed or someone's robbed.
Everyone else will play the game,
You fall apart."

He's thinking of the old days as he walks by the stream,
Thinking of a wasted life and all those shattered dreams,
All those shattered dreams . . .

They said to him: "Just close your eyes!
Forget the damned, forget their cries,
Time will be taking care of that,
You should comply."

But he wouldn't listen to their pleas –
He chose the freedom of the seas,
Now he's just a face in a foreign land,
He's become a refugee.

He's thinking of the old days as he walks by the stream,
Thinking of a wasted life and all those shattered dreams,
All those shattered dreams . . .

Shusha

Don't Speak Don't Wish Don't Expect

After my bath
after warming up
I caress myself.
I pull my breast.
I sweat.
I have a bath.
After I warm up
I caress myself.
I pull my breast.
I think about a bridge
I will jump from when I am happy.
Then I fall asleep.
I awaken.
After warming up
I write. A letter or something
like this.
In my thoughts
I have a bath.
I caress myself
in my thoughts. I think
that all the caressing
and bathing and sleeping
come from you

but you are not in touch.
I fall asleep.
I caress myself
in my dream.

Ifigenija Simonovic

Burning Roses

Father I am burning roses
father only God shall know
what the secret heart discloses
the ancient dances with the doe

Father I have sorely wounded
father I shall wound no more
I have waltzed among the thorns
where roses burn upon the floor

Daughter may you turn in laughter
a candle dreams a candle draws
the heart that burns
shall burn thereafter
may you turn as roses fall

Patti Smith

Patti Smith

Farewell Reel
In Memory of Fred Sonic Smith

It's been a hard time
and when it rains
it rains on me
the sky just opens
and when it rains
it pours

I walk alone
assaulted it seems
by tears from heaven
and darling I can't
help thinking those
tears are yours

Our wild love came from above
and wilder still
is the wind that howls
like a voice that knows it's gone
cause darling you died
and well I cried
but I'll get by
salute our love
and send you a smile
and move on

So darling farewell
all will be well
the children will rise
strong and happy be sure
cause your love flows
and the corn still grows
and God only knows
we're only given
as much as the heart can endure

But I don't know why
but when it rains
it rains on me
the sky just opens
and when it rains
it pours

But I look up
and a rainbow appears
like a smile from heaven
and darling I can't
help thinking that smile
is yours

In Memoriam:
Dr Timothy Leary LSD

So. Farewell
Then
Dr Timothy
Leary.

Sixties guru
And advocate of
Mind-Expanding
Drugs.

"Turn on,
Tune in,
Drop out."

That was
Your catchphrase.

Keith says
Now it should
Be
"Drop Dead."

Personally I
Think Keith
Has dropped
Too much
Acid.

M-a-a-a-n.

June 1996

In Memoriam:
Dizzy Gillespie and
Rudolf Nureyev

So. Farewell
Then
Dizzy Gillespie
Famous jazz
Trumpeter.

You were known
For your
Bulging cheeks.

Rudolf Nureyev.

So were
You.

January 1993

E J Thribb (17½)

Andrei Voznesensky

The prisoners make the seat-covers for Aeroflot.
My flights are solidly based on their crimes,
both minor and terrible. The prisoners
sew the material for the seats from strong cloth,
so that we can catapult into flight.
I cannot sleep in the section with the blinds down.
A rapist bit this thread with his teeth.
A framed woman prisoner ruined her eyesight.
Prisoners sew the seat-covers for Aeroflot.
I pray for an unknown woman prisoner,
who swore as she sewed this chair-cover for me.
Oh Lord has she died or is she risen again?
Sky. Freedom. Thighs of the Gods.
Prisoners sew the seat-covers for Aeroflot.

trs: Richard McKane

Wiper – Weep

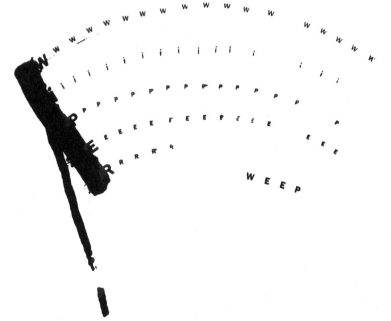

Andrei Voznesensky

Abductee

written as a song in collaboration with Martin Wilkinson

I was walking on the beach in the middle of the night
Picking my way through the rocks in the silver light
I wanted a UFO to take me away
To take me away for a thousand-year day.

I want to be an abductee
I want to be free, supernaturally
I want star light in my veins
I want star light in my brains.

Like a bubble in a bottle, trying to escape
I feel trapped on earth with its restless lies
I feel like cracking up beneath the weight
I want to fizz out, and dematerialise.

I want strange tendrils to sink in my brain
Then water my soul with cosmic rain
I want to be flung out into the sky
I want to fly without having to try.

The old blue light of Earth was fading tragically
A dying cell, cold and alone . . .
I saw a reason to leave immediately
And slip away through the frail ozone

As the earth's heart was beginning to break
I was being seduced by the shimmering stars
Hypnotised by signals from the Milky Way
Sirius, Saturn and the Moons of Mars.

Weird force fields were round my face
I was stolen away from all that pain
A voice told me "never look back again,
If you do you're sure to lose pace."

All shook up by the quantum dance
I was raving in a rainbow trance
My soul was floating, floating free
Home at last in zero gravity.

Heathcote Williams

I was astro-surfing on solar wind
An Earth Angel sailing through the void
Buzzing like a pinball in the heavenly mind
A human electron, a living asteroid.

Sucked into the centre of an imploded star
You weigh a billion tons – it doesn't matter who you are
Suddenly, a vortex makes you lighter than light
Flashing like a firework through the everlasting night.

Re-tuned by golden laser beams
That radiate from crystal streams
I could travel back and forth in time
Relativity was just a nursery rhyme

I turned into a million mile streak
Of spectral dust and stellar gas
The light in my head fused with all the light in space
My body dissolved and disappeared without trace

Stars fire like nerve cells in a mega-brain
I hear ecstatic notes from the music of the spheres
Why read your stars when you've got stars in your face?
– Whispering out the future in your ears

I saw the specks of light with which I see
Could be the light from unborn galaxies
When you're lit up with inner fire
The Universe itself is the Messiah

I want to be an abductee
I want to be free supernaturally
I want star light in my veins
I want star light in my brains . . .

I want to be an abductee
I want to be free supernaturally
When you're lit up with inner fire
The Universe itself is the Messiah

Heathcote Williams

Jah Wobble

I LOVE EVERYBODY

AND NOW THE BUILDINGS CHANGE. NOW THE PEOPLE CHANGE. EVERYTHING CHANGING. SPIRIT IN MATTER MOST APPARENT. REALISED THERE NEVER WAS ANYTHING TO WORRY ABOUT, TO DOUBT WAS INSANE. THE LIMITED, CALLOW, ISOLATED INDIVIDUALS LIVING ON HOUSING ESTATES IN CHINGFORD, LARGE DETACHED HOUSES IN KEW, TOWER BLOCKS ON THE TOTTENHAM MARSHES, BECOME MY GODS. I SEE AN ACCOUNTS CLERK FROM TOOTING, I SEE ZEUS. A SANITARY INSPECTOR FROM THE LONDON BOROUGH OF HARINGEY, AND BRAHMIN STANDS RESPLENDENT BEFORE ME. FOR 5 MINUTES I LOVE EVERYBODY. THERE IS ONLY LOVE, ALL ACTION CEASES. THE MILE END ROAD, ONCE A BLOOD-STAINED BATTLEFIELD OF BACCHANALIAN EXCESS, BECOMES THE GARDEN OF GETHSEMANE. A BITTER, 72 YEAR OLD EX-DOCKER BECOMES THE EVER COMPASSIONATE BUDDHA. A CYPRIOT MINICAB DRIVER BECOMES ST FRANCIS OF ASSISI. THE 22 YEAR OLD GLASWEGIAN CHECKOUT GIRL IS THE DIVINE MOTHER. I LOVE EVERYBODY. MY SPIRIT IS FREE. I AM LIMITLESS IN SPACE, TIME AND MATTER, SIMULTANEOUSLY THE PLANET NEPTUNE, PART OF THE STRUCTURAL SUPPORT TO VAUXHALL BBRIDGE. I AM YOUR LEFT BREAST, I AM STEPNEY, I AM PERU, I AM DIVINE AND SO ARE YOU. I LOVE EVERYBODY. I AM NOTHING EXCEPT A MERE CLUSTER OF NOTES, A ROAD SIGN IN SKELMERSDALE. I RAN THE ROMAN EMPIRE. I WAS A LAVATORY ATTENDANT IN HULL. I AM EVERYBODY AND EVERYBODY IS ME. SPIRIT. WHO PUT THE SPIRIT IN MATTER? LOVE.

Jah Wobble

NO CHANGE IS SEXY

LET'S NOT CHANGE THE WORLD, LEAVE IT LIKE IT IS. NO CHANGE, NO CHANGE IS SEXY. LET'S NOT LOOK INSIDE FOR INNER WORLDS, LET'S NOT FIND MEANING, REASONS TO CHANGE. CHANGE IS BAD, NO CHANGE IS SEXY. LET'S LOSE OURSELVES IN DRIVES FROM RUGBY TO HULL, HORNCHURCH TO GANT'S HILL, WALLSEND TO GLAMORGAN. LET'S BE SEXY. LET'S TALK OF TAKING OUR LIVES AS IF CONSIDERING A TRIP TO THE VIDEO SHOP, "YEAH I MIGHT TOP MYSELF LATER. I'LL SEE HOW I FEEL. I'LL NEVER SEE THE RAINFOREST ANYWAY." LET'S MAKE JOKES ABOUT MURDERING SHOP ASSISTANTS AND EATING THEIR LIVERS WITH VIRGIN OLIVE OIL AND A SPRIG OF PARSLEY. NO CHANGE IS SEXY. LET'S WALK AROUND SUPERMARKETS AND GET TURNED ON BY THE TWISTED AND CONTORTED FACES OF PEOPLE DOING THEIR SHOPPING. LET'S MAKE LOVE SURROUNDED BY THE DISTRESS SIGNALS OF BROWN PAPER TAKEAWAY BAGS AND PORNOGRAPHIC VIDEOS. ROMEO AND JULIET IN A PASSIONATE COMPULSIVITY. BLEAK IS A HAPPENER, AND NO CHANGE IS SEXY. NO, LET'S NOT CHANGE THE WORLD. LET'S BECOME AROUSED BY THE ACRID AROMA OF URINE IN A DEEP TUNNEL UNDERGROUND STATION. "YOU'LL NEVER SEE THE RAINFOREST ANYWAY." I LOVE THIS SOCIETY. I KNOW WHERE I AM. NO CHANGE IS SEXY. LET'S FORGET ANGRY ALLIANCES, ENDLESSLY REPLAYING SCENES OF REJECTION AND VIOLATION. TO CHANGE IS BAD. CHANGE IS A MISNOMER, PROMOTED BY CALIFORNIANS WITH STRANGE HAIRCUTS AND SYMMETRICAL TEETH. CHANGE DOESN'T TURN ME ON. LET'S GO TO A LAYBY ON THE NORTH CIRCULAR AND PLACE PLASTIC BAGS OVER OUR HEADS, SMASH MASONRY NAILS THROUGH OUR ANKLES, WHILST HUMMING THE THEME TUNE TO 'BONANZA'. OR WAS IT 'THE HIGH CHAPPARAL'? NO CHANGE MAKES ME SULTRY. I LOVE NO CHANGE. I AM THAT THAT AM I.

I Found South African Breweries Most Hospitable

Meat smell of blood in locked rooms I cannot smell it,
Screams of the brave in torture loges I never heard nor heard of
Apartheid I wouldn't know how to spell it,
None of these things am I paid to believe a word of
For I am a stranger to cant and contumely.
I am a professional cricketer
My only consideration is my family.

I get my head down nothing to me or mine
Blood is geysering now from ear, from mouth, from eye,
How they take a fresh guard after breaking the spine,
I must play wherever I like or die
So spare me your news your views spare me your homily.
I am a professional cricketer.
My only consideration is my family.

Electrodes wired to their brains they should have had helmets,
Balls wired up they should have been wearing a box,
The danger was the game would turn into a stalemate,
Skin of their feet burnt off I like thick woollen socks
With buckskin boots that accommodate them roomily
For I am a professional cricketer.
My only consideration is my family.

They keep falling out of the window they must be clumsy
And unprofessional not that anyone told me,
Spare me your wittering spare me your whimsy,
Sixty thousand pounds is what they sold me
And I have no brain. I am an anomaly.
I am a professional cricketer.
My only consideration is my family.

Kit Wright

Rock Around the Wok

There's a frying and a frizzling
    and a simmer and a sizzling
    in the WOK . . .

There's a bunch o' crazy beanshoots
    and the shoots are pretty meanshoots
    in the WOK . . .

There's a ginger root a-jumping
    and a lotta stalks a-stumping
    in the WOK . . .

There's onions that are springing
    and there's flavours that are singing
    in the WOK . . .

    So,
    Baby,

    LET'S GO STIR THE WOK
    (Oh, baby)
    LET'S GO STIR THE WOK
    (Oh, baby)
    ROCK AROUND THE WOK

        Because:

        There's a lotta food,
           There's a lotta heat.
        So shake it up!
           That's enough.
        Let's eat

        FROM THE WOK!

Kit Wright

Notes on the Contributors

Mervyn Africa

The leader of Zila (who are working with the acappella quartet Progress at the SuperJam), Africa came to Britain in 1981 and co-founded the Afro-Jazz group District 6, named after the notorious area of Capetown in which he was raised. He's a prolific composer, bandleader and player, synthesising township, kwela, jazz and European roots. His distinctively percussive piano technique has its origins in the repetitive rhythmic patterns of the South African *Mbira* (African precursor of the piano).
(Photo: Bob Huntbach)

John Agard

Agard left Guyana in 1977 and swiftly became a leading light in the suddenly exploding galaxy of West Indian-British troubadours, hilarious and moving by turns, with sharply satiric intelligence conjuring delighted audiences of children and adults to join in. His books include *Lovelines for a Goat-born Lady* (Serpent's Tail 1990) and *Laughter is an Egg* (Viking 1990), and a healthy dose of Agard is featured in the *Grandchildren of Albion* anthology (New Departures 1992).

Patience Agbabi

One of the youngest voices on the SuperJam, Agbabi is Nigerian and British, and blends elements from rap, punk, ska and blues in her skanking performances. Benjamin Zephaniah regards her first collection, *R.A.W.* (Gecko Press 1995), as "only more proof that great performance poetry can bring to the page that raw, wicked stuff that has brought British poetry back to life . . . and a self-portrait of a poet whose honesty, intelligence and wit gives poets like me someone to look up to."

Africa   Agard   Agbabi

Damon Albarn

Albarn, charismatic singer-lyricist-keyboardist apotheosis of Essex Boy, projects a style which strikes perfect accord with the *Poetry Olympics*/New Departures platforms, extending the same broad counter-cultural network his parents engineered (Mum was a stage designer for Joan Littlewood, Dad helped catalyse the London underground arts [r]evolution, worked with Soft Machine and is still head of design at Colchester Institute). As Neil Spencer put it in a recent *Observer*, the "leader of Blur, teenage pin-up, inspiration of 1990s Britpop . . . he's as near the spirit of the age as any contender." (Photo: Steve Pyke)

Simon Armitage

Simon Armitage was born in Huddersfield in 1963 and now works as a probation officer in Oldham. *Zoom!* (1989) was one of the most acclaimed first collections of the 1980s, and he followed it with *Kid* (Faber), as slangy, downbeat and witty as his début, and *Xanadu* (Bloodaxe), the poems written to accompany a film that he made for television about a Rochdale Housing Estate. Peter Reading has written that ". . . Armitage creates a muscular but elegant language of his own out of youthful, up-to-the-minute jargon and the vernacular of his native northern England. He combines this with an easily worn erudition, plenty of nous and the benefit of unblinkered experience . . . to produce poems of moving originality." (Photo: Jason Bell)

Sujata Bhatt

Bhatt's mind-stilling poems explore mythic landscapes, scientific laboratories, racism and the interaction of Asian, European and North American cultures – the dilemma of having "two tongues in your mouth." She has translated Gujarati verse for the Penguin anthology of *Contemporary Indian Women Poets*, and her three collections from Carcanet, *Brunizen* (1988), *Monkey Shadows* (1991) and *The Stinking Rose* (1995) have been duly acknowledged with numerous major prizes and unreserved encomia from her peers. Sujata is also prominent in *Grandchildren of Albion* and the *Grandchildren of Albion Live* cassette and CD recordings (New Departures 1992/1995/1996).

James Berry

Growing up in Jamaica, Berry felt as much disturbed by his African
background as by the European slave-trade and its aftermath.
His scintillating anthology *News for Babylon* (Chatto & Windus 1984)
brought the new dawn of Anglo-Caribbean bards home to the
mainstream readership, and his latest volume, *Hot Earth Cold Earth*
(Bloodaxe 1995), shows him writing at the height of his powers at
the age of 70. Stewart Brown thinks of his poetry as "celebration with
an echo of despair." (Photo: Christine Voge)

Valerie Bloom

Her uniquely entertaining yet devastating pitch salts English poetic
forms with pungent Jamaican *patwa*. Linton Kwesi Johnson has noted
her ". . . ironical penchant for farcical situations, her skilful character
sketches, her mastery of form and language . . . an important and
welcome addition to an ever-growing body of Caribbean oral poetry,
whose new voices have largely eschewed the inherited colonial literary
tradition." Her books include *Touch Mi! Tell Mi!* (Bogle l'Ouverture
1982) and *Duppy Jamboree* (Cambridge 1992) – which demonstrates
her rapport with children of all ages. She is another of the palpably
read-outable *Grandchildren of Albion* (NDs 1992).

The Broadside Band

Whenever the Broadside Band bounce into their recordings and concerts
of ballads, country dances and popular music of the 17th and 18th
Centuries, they delight audiences and critics alike. Between them, the
musicians – Jeremy Barlow, Alastair McLachlan, Rosemary
Thorndycraft and George Weigand – play a multitude of instruments,
including lute, flute, hurdy-gurdy, violin, virginals, pipe and tabor.
On the SuperJam they'll also accompany Evelyn Tubb in settings of
Shakespeare songs, including 'Full Fathome Five' (see page 61).

Eliza and Martin Carthy

Martin Carthy cut his musical teeth during the postwar skiffle boom
and is reckoned by most of his fellows to be the greatest modern
interpreter of English folksong, and the guitarist's guitarist. His daughter
by Norma Waterson, Eliza, plays guitar, mandolin and fiddle, and is
seen as "the brightest star to emerge in recent years with the talent and
vision to take the music forward into the next decade and beyond."
They will be joined by Norma Waterson on the SuperJam for a Waterson
: Carthy set, for which lovers of their many gigs and albums will need no
further recommendation. Bruce Elder came away from a recent concert
in Sydney feeling ". . . reconnected by the beauty of the voices and
the marvellous originality of the playing, with that great English liberal
humanitarian tradition which reaches back to Shakespeare and Chaucer,
which has been so crudely attacked and damaged by self-seeking
ignorance."

Nina Cassian

Savagely sensual and incisively humourous, Cassian's poems and
readings are as high-spirited as they are hard-hitting. After 55 years in
Romania, she was lucky enough to be in the USA when some verses
lampooning the Ceaucescus were found in a friend's diary – the friend
was tortured to death. Cassian has stayed based in New York, and
speaks of "my tongue – forked like a snake's in/to a bilingual hissing."
Her latest book in English (translated by herself with Brenda Walker,
Forest Books 1992), is *Cheerleader for a Funeral*. (Photo: Ian Evans)

Nick Cave

Born in Australia in 1957, Cave achieved early recognition as a founding member of the rock group The Birthday Party. His novel *And the Ass Saw the Angel* (Penguin 1989) and his bran-tub collection of lyrics and poems *King Ink* (Black Spring Press 1989) supplement a prolific stream of recordings and gigs with the Bad Seeds. His latest album is *Murder Ballads* (Mute Records 1996). His chanting poems will be accompanied on the SuperJam by the virtuoso violin and piano-accordion playing of Warren Ellis.

John Cooper Clarke

Clarke is widely regarded as Britain's leading rock poet. His Manchester Motormouth delivery, streetwise humour, Betjemanesque chants, lyrics and laments for commercial travellers and provincial seaside urbanales issue – as he puts it himself – "the slang anthems of the zip age in the desperate esperanto of bop." In Tom Paulin's words, his work "belongs to the popular and populist oral tradition that amplifies a singing consciousness as it moves from primeval woodland, through complaints about enclosures, to industrial ballads and modern songs which mention fish fingers. Like many of these anonymous poets, Clarke writes a form of native pidgin or English Creole, with a throbbing and exultantly dionysiac wildness." Clarke's extraordinary voice and phrasing can be sampled on many recordings including the first *Poetry Olympics* LP, and also, in the mind's ear, on the pages of *Grandchildren of Albion* (New Departures).

Ray Davies

Acclaimed "Godfather of British pop", Davies achieved worldwide impact since he first exploded onto the music scene in the early 1960s. His first number-one hit single *You Really Got Me* was followed by 30 albums and a series of hit singles he wrote for the Kinks, including such classics of pop songwriting as *Waterloo Sunset*, *Lola*, *Dedicated Follower of Fashion*, *Well Respected Man* and *Sunny Afternoon*. He has composed pioneering rock operas and written, directed and appeared in a number of films and plays. Since publishing his "Unauthorized Autobiography", *X-Ray*, last year (Penguin), Ray has been touring internationally with his one-man show, *20th Century Man*.

Cave   Cooper Clarke   Davies

Carol Ann Duffy

Born in Glasgow, Duffy spent her childhood in Staffordshire, studied
Philosophy at Liverpool University, and now lives in London. Her highly
original verse received massive readership and an extraordinary number
of awards. Robert Nye welcomed her first major volume, *Standing
Female Nude* (Anvil 1985), for its "clarity, a mixture of charm and
truthfulness which breaks the windows of perception in new ways
altogether", whilst Peter Porter wrote, ". . . It is good to see a crusading
spirit refusing to surrender any touch of art to the urgency of its cause."
Her most recent publications have been with Anvil and Penguin
Modern Poets. (Photo: Neil Mayell)

Paul Durcan

Durcan was born in Dublin in 1944
of County Mayo parents, and studied
archaeology and medieval history
at University College, Cork. He has
published fourteen books of poems,
of which *A Snail in My Prime: New
and Selected Poems* (Harvill Press,
1993) is probably the best
introduction. His performances are
famously mesmerising. Carol Ann
Duffy says, ". . . To have heard him
adds another pleasure to the reading
of his work – but the voice speaks
clearly on the page in poems of
harrowing intimacy, politics and
love. He holds a mirror up to himself:
but we can see ourselves over
his shoulder, whoever we are."
(Photo: Caroline Forbes)

Warren Ellis

The Dirty Three, fronted by virtuoso guitarist and piano-accordion
player Warren, are regarded as founding fathers of Aussie punk.
According to *Rolling Stone*, Ellis is "the Jimi Hendrix of his
instrument." Everett True wrote of Warren's performance at
Rotterdam's Nighttown in 1995 that his playing was ". . . positively
infernal; so wild, so wanton, so wondrous are his sweeps of the bow
and screeching exhortations. I'm reminded of euphoric Gallic dances
and star-kissed Greek evenings round the camp fire with a grateful
of Ouzo." (Photo: Nigel Cox)

James Fenton

Recently elected Professor of Poetry at Oxford University, Fenton has worked variously as a political and literary journalist, a freelance reporter in Indo-China, a reporter in Germany for the *Guardian*, literary editor of the *Sunday Times*, chief book reviewer for the *Times* and, from 1986-88, Southeast Asia correspondent for the *Independent*. His first collection of poems since *The Memory of War & Children in Exile* (Penguin 1983) was *Out of Danger* (Penguin 1993). Peter Porter thinks Fenton "the most talented poet of his generation."

Justine Frischmann

Justine Frischmann, singer-guitarist with Elastica, was one of the MCs on *A Hip Mass: The SuperJam*. "Line Up" is one of several cool yet searing songs contributed by her to Elastica's first album, *Elastica*, on the Bluff/Deceptive label.

Ian Hall

Born in British Guyana, educated at Oxford (the first Black person to take an Honours Degree in Music there), he has enriched ecclesiastical music as composer, conductor, organist and singer. The legacy of his incumbency as organist and Director of Music at the University of London Church (aged 26) is the alembic of the Bloomsbury International Society, for the advancement of racial harmony through the arts. He has recently composed and conducted music for the 50th anniversary of the United Nations, celebrated in New York's Cathedral of St John the Divine.

John Hegley

This one-off fringe comedian and poet-singer-songwriter-guitarist has been captivating audiences everywhere for 25 years. He began his cabaret career at London's notoriously tough Comedy Store, and is a laureate of the kind of subject matter most poets throw away. Thus the larger fraction of his first full-length collection, *Glad to Wear Glasses* (Deutsch 1990), is indeed about little else but glasses.

Hegley   Hall   Frischmann   Fenton

Miroslav Holub

Ted Hughes considers Holub "one of the half-dozen most important poets writing anywhere." He's also one of the Czech Republic's most distinguished scientists, an immunologist who brings to his writing the notion of "a discovery which is going to stay" and a trust in "concreteness as the counterweight to a lie": a notion and a trust which have survived the oppressive régimes which tried to throttle their open expression. Holub's main translator into English, Ewald Osers, notes that "... What is conspicuous in Holub's work is the Czech *Soldier Svejk* tradition, that typically Czech trait of poking gentle fun at authority, at unquestioningly accepted notions, and at taking oneself too seriously." The latest Holub sequence is *Supposed to Fly* (Bloodaxe 1996). (Photo: Moira Conway)

Michael Horovitz

Pioneer of jazz poetry with Stan Tracey et al since 1960, Horovitz is characterised by Allen Ginsberg as a "popular, experienced, experimental, New Jerusalem, Jazz Generation, Sensitive Bard." Horovitz has put the Poetry Olympics Weekend (POW!) festival of 5–7 July 1996 together as a farewell-to-large-scale-organising party, and also in order to redeem and extend the three venues (Poets' Corner, The Tabernacle and the Royal Albert Hall) for poetry as Temples of the Muses. He's spent most of his adult life as a poet, singer-songwriter, jazz and blues kazooist, clown, impresario, visual artist, translator, literary journalist and editor-publisher (mainly of New Departures publications). His poetry books in print are *Midsummer Morning Jog Log*, a 700-line rural rhapsody illustrated by Peter Blake (Five Seasons Press 1986), and *Wordsounds & Sightlines: New & Selected Poems* (Sinclair-Stevenson 1994). (Photo: Alfred Benjamin)

Nerys Hughes

One of Britain's most popular actresses, known to millions as Sandra in *The Liverbirds* and as *The District Nurse*, Nerys broadcasts regularly on radio and has made many recordings, including an all-star version of Dylan Thomas's *Under Milk Wood* directed by Sir Anthony Hopkins. Originally from Rhyl, she's written columns for *Wales on Sunday* et al, and is currently presenting on *Capital Woman* for ITV. The SuperJam selections she's performing from *Under Milk Wood* with the New Stan Tracey Quartet are a first-time collaboration (we felt it was time the play was voiced from a completely female angle – and whose voice and person better than Nerys's to pitch it?).

Holub   Horovitz   Hughes

Mahmood Jamal

Mahmood Jamal was born in Lucknow, India in 1948. His family migrated to Pakistan in the early 1950s and came to Britain in 1967. He edited and translated the *Penguin Book of Urdu Verse* (1986), and has also scripted, produced and directed many music, drama and documentary films, mainly for Channel 4. His poetry books are *Coins for Charon* (Courtfield Press 1976), and *Silence Inside a Gun's Mouth* (Kala Press 1984).

Marina Kalmikova

Marina Kalmikova, 33, is a Russian stage and screen actress from Riga, Latvia. An accomplished guitarist, she sings poems by Akhmatova, Lorca, Mandelshtam and others, set to her own music. She has recently added Shakespeare's 40th Sonnet to her repertoire. She is married to Igor Khokhlovkin, a stage director; the couple make a formidable team, writing and broadcasting programmes on leading Russian poets and writers. A recent programme *Esenin Abroad* won high praise, and was broadcast to Russia by the Russian Service of the BBC. Marina is a passionate  interpreter of the traditional songs of the Russian gypsies. A natural blond, she has recently dyed her hair a gypsy black to feel her way into the part.

Jackie Kay

Born in Edinburgh in 1961, Kay grew up in Glasgow and now lives with her son in London where she's a freelance writer. She has written a number of plays, collections of poetry for children, and the beautiful poetry volumes *The Adoption Papers* (Bloodaxe 1991) and *Other Lovers* (Bloodaxe 1993). Her television output includes film on pornography, AIDS and transracial adoption. Her performances convey great tenderness, generosity, humour and commitment to everyone in the audience.

Jamal   Kalmikova   Kay

Brendan Kennelly

After his shocking epic poem *Cromwell* and the even more shocking *Book of Judas*, Kennelly's *Poetry My Arse!* (Bloodaxe 1995) brilliantly debunks the intellectual élitism often associated with poets and poetry. Kennelly is a prolific writer and distinguished professor at Trinity College, Dublin – yet has always represented the salt of the earth. It would seem his popularity (his books regularly top the Irish bestsellers lists) resides in his concern with specifics and with common humanity – as he's said, ". . . Poetry must always be a flight from deadening authoritative egotism and must find its voices in the byways, laneways, backyards, nooks and crannies of self." U2's Bono sings the praises of Brendan's ". . . poetry as base as heavy metal, as high as the Holy Spirit flies, comic and tragic, from litany to rant, roaring at times, soaring at other times. Like David in the Psalms, like Robert Johnson in the blues, the poet scratches out Screwtape letters to a God who may or may not have abandoned him, and of course to anyone else who is listening." (Photo: Ian Ground)

Hanif Kureishi

Kureishi was born in Bromley in 1954 to an English mother and Pakistani father. His films *My Beautiful Laundrette* and *Sammy and Rosie Get Laid*, like the novels *The Buddha of Suburbia* and *The Black Album* (all from Faber) have outraged and delighted readers, audiences and critics in more or less equal measure. According to the *Observer*, Kureishi is "incapable of creating a dull or hackneyed character. Add to that his fresh vision of empire's aftermath and his flair for pop culture, and it's plain to see why Colin McCabe hails him as 'one of the great talents of the last 25 years'." (Photo: Nigel Parry)

Inge Elsa Laird

Born in Germany of Hungarian and Jewish ancestry, Laird has lived and worked mainly in the UK since 1962, writing minimalist poetry, prose and translations published in the *Financial Times*, *Jewish Chronicle*, *New Departures*, *Books* etc. She is co-editor of *New Departures*, and co-organiser of Poetry Olympics, in addition to working as an interpreter/ translator.

Kennelly   Kureishi   Laird

Fran Landesman

Fran's song lyrics such as *Ballad of the Sad Young Men* and *Spring can really hang you up the most* have been sung by most of the finest singers of the last 30 years, but her own performances of her poetry are something else again. Alan Massie wrote of an Edinburgh gig, ". . . Her performance has a cool self-deprecating charm. She seems to me wittier and truer than Sondheim – rhythmical, alert, sensitive." Her latest selection, *Rhymes at Midnight* (Golden Handshake 1996) provoked this from Ned Sherrin: "Midnight? I could read or listen to Fran Landesman's funny, elegant, wise lyrics right around the clock." Take *Deeply Shallow*: ". . . I'm looking for a meaningless relationship/ With a deeply shallow man/ Passion with its awful fascination skip/ That isn't in my plan/ . . . I just can't take the sleepless nights and all that shit/ I've escaped love's frying pan/ Now I only want to mess around a little bit/ With a deeply shallow/ (This may be hard to swallow)/ But I'm looking for a deeply shallow man." (Photo: Maryrose Story)

Gwyneth Lewis

Lewis writes in her first language, Welsh, and also in English. Her prize-winning first volume *Parables and Faxes* (Bloodaxe 1995) won immediate transatlantic response. For the late Joseph Brodsky, her poems, "felicitous, urbane, heartbreaking ... form a universe whose planets use language for oxygen and thus are inhabitable." For Peter Porter, "Her Welsh/English pendulum swings warmly across worlds as separate as the rural communities of Wales and the academic palisades of Britain and America. The extended title sequence is the most humane and mysterious succession of poems I've read for many years – it is simply a masterpiece."

Christopher Logue

Logue began publishing his poetry in the early 1950s in Paris, and on his return to London he wrote plays and a musical for the Royal Court, recorded *Red Bird Dancing on Ivory* with Tony Kinsey's jazz combo, and experimented with poster and collage poems. Logue's eloquent readings transmit his belief in poetry as a social force – dissident, sensual, humourous – as does his continuing translation of Homer's *Iliad* (dubbed "the best since Pope's" by the *New York Review of Books*). His *Selected Poems* have just been published by Faber. He will be reading from his Homer at the *International Poetry Prelude* at Poets' Corner, Westminster Abbey, on Friday 5th July; and along with Horovitz, Mitchell and Voznesensky, Logue is one of those reading at Royal Albert Hall on Sunday 7th July who also read at the First International Poetry Incarnation in the Hall in 1965.
(Photo: Rosemary Hill)

Roger McGough

One of the bestselling and most popular poets alive, with both children and adults in his thrall, McGough remains as constantly alert and developing as ever. Since the Penguin *Mersey Sound* of 1967 to the latest Penguin Modern Poets volume of last year, he has gone on delivering good advice and uncomfortable perspectives. *Defying Gravity* (Penguin 1995) sparkles with no diminution of verbal dexterity, irreverent wit or heartfelt compassion. As Charles Causley says, "A word juggler who never misses a catch."

Adrian Mitchell

The simplicity, clarity, passion and humour of Mitchell's verse display his allegiance to the vital popular tradition that embraces William Blake, the Border Ballads and the blues. His most nakedly political poems – about nuclear war, prisons and racism – are part of the folklore of the Left, sung and recited at demonstrations and mass rallies. Angela Carter described him as a "joyous, acrid and demotic tumbling Pied Piper determinedly singing us away from catastrophe." His latest book, *Blue Coffee: Poems 1985–1996* (Bloodaxe 1996) is a Poetry Book Society Choice. Long ago he wrote a *Stunted Sonnet*: "Love is like a cigarette – / The bigger the drag, the more you get." But now his poems of smokeless love breathe pure light.

Moondog

Born Louis Hardin in Kansas in 1916 and blinded by an industrial accident at 16, Moondog got his first musical training at Iowa School for the Blind. Strongly influenced by Indian drumbeats and European classical music, his timeless compositions are overlaid with percussive rhythms and formal beauty. In 1949 he started playing drums in New York shop-doorways at night, and fashioned his own instruments so that they fitted that unusual venue. In 1952 he made his first recording, *On the Streets of New York*, incorporating amongst much else a duet with the horn of the Queen Elizabeth as it docked. He's made many recordings in all sorts of contexts since, including a 1969 Columbia album with a 40-piece symphony orchestra performing his works. The catalogue of this unsung genius's work numbers 81 symphonies, 16 "Troikans", many songs, over 1,000 poems. His public appearances are all too rare, and for the SuperJam he plans to "kick up a storm . . ." (Photo: Phil Starling)

McGough   Mitchell   Moondog

Mulatni

Mulatni will play a violin invention which draws on the musical experience of its members and was co-devised especially for tonight's event launching the first Poetry Olympics Weekend. **Fiona Barrow** trained classically and has since diversified into playing a wide cross-section of music leading to extensive performing opportunities in Britain and Europe. **B K Chandrashekar** is presently a teacher of Karnatic (South Indian Classical) violin at BHAVAN Institute of Indian Culture (London), a prolific composer of contemporary dance ballads and South Indian film music and a seasoned performer, both as a solo artist and, recently, in collaborations with The Cure and Nitin Sawnhey, among others. **Ben Constantine** trained at the RCM (London) and has played internationally, specialising in the authentic performance of Baroque music. **Joe Townsend**'s fired-up playing, inspired by music from Eastern Europe, Celtic roots and Jazz, has led to performances in Poland, Romania, Ireland, America and Japan. He is currently working at the Royal National Theatre (London), playing music in films and in concerts with his own band, The Diablo Strings. **Ruth Vaughn** is a performer who combines an interest in text with studying Karnatic violin and playing East European "dance house" with the Doppelganger Gypsy Orchestra.

Grace Nichols

Grace Nichols worked in her native Guyana as a journalist before coming to Britain in 1977. She has published many children's books, anthologies and novels. Her cycle *i is a long memoried woman* (Karnac House 1983) won several prizes including the Commonwealth Poetry Prize, and each succeeding volume has earned her a more inspired readership. As Gwendolyn Brooks wrote, we get ". . . Not only rich music, an easy lyricism, but also grit and earthy honesty, a willingness to be vulnerable and clean." *Sunris: New Poems*, her fourth collection, appears this summer from Virago. Representative selections from her earlier poetry grace the *Grandchildren of Albion* anthology and also the *Grandchildren of Albion Live* cassette and CD (New Departures). (Photo: Sheila Gerachti)

Ben Okri

Ben Okri has published ten books including *The Famished Road*, which won the Booker Prize in 1991, *Songs of Enchantment* and *Astonishing the Gods*. He has also published a collection of poems, *An African Elegy*. He has been a Fellow Commoner in Creative Arts at Trinity College, Cambridge. *The Famished Road* received some of the most poetically entranced reviews any narrative can ever have received. Linda Grant's response, for instance, concluded, "Okri is incapable of writing

a boring sentence. As one startling image follows the next,
The Famished Road begins to read like an epic poem that happens to
touch down just this side of prose. Beside it, most modern British fiction
seems deracinated and condemned to the worst sort of literalness . . .
When I finished this book and went outside, it was as if all the trees in
South London had angels sitting in them" (*The Independent*). Ben Okri's
books have won several awards including lhe Commonwealth Writers'
Prize for Africa. In 1995 the World Economic Forum presented Ben Okri
with the Crystal Award for his outstanding contribution to the arts and
to cross-cultural understanding. Ben Okri was born in Nigeria and now
lives in London. (Photo: The Douglas Brothers)

Gerard Presencer

Though still in his early twenties, Presencer is widely regarded as one of
the most accomplished jazz trumpet and flugelhorn players in the world.
He'll be featured on Stan Tracey's setting of *Under Milk Wood* with the
voicings of Nerys Hughes.

Progress

The South African all-female acappella group Progress was formed by
Pinise Saul in 1990 and has swiftly become vastly popular for its
marvellous mix of South African folk, contemporary, soul, gospel, blues
and township. The singers are Pinise Saul, Julia Mathunjwa, Ruby
Matshidiso Morare and Nomsa Caiuza. They are usually accompanied
by the rhythm section Zila. (Photo: Graham de Smith)

Lucky Ranku

Lucky became a prominent constituent of Dudu Pukwana's Zila, and more so after the founder's untimely death. His virtuoso guitar style is uniquely his own, but unmistakably South African. He's toured and performed with Chris McGregor, Songs of Soweto, Steve Arguelles, Jazz Africa and Shikisha.

Pinise Saul

Saul came to London from South Africa with the musical Ipi Ntombi. She gained an immediate following singing with the Brotherhood of Breath, Johnny Dyani, Trevor Watts' Moire Music, Jabula and Dudu Pukwana's Zila. She sang in the Nelson Mandela concerts at Wembley and founded both Progress and the South African Gospel Choir, Mohobelo. Her voice is soulful – rich and assured, sometimes pained, often strong and sweet – "like fire", one listener said, "eating through honey."

Kazuko Shiraishi

Born in Vancouver, Kazuko was taken to Japan just before World War II, and her first poetry, written in her late teens, emerged from the violence and ugliness of postwar Tokyo. She developed a talent for vivid, bizarre imagery, and gradually got involved with modern jazz and the performance of her wordsounds, dramatising a society of alienation where music and poetry seem the only values and sex the prime solace. The title of her main collection in English, *Seasons of Sacred Lust* (edited by Kenneth Rexroth, New Directions 1975) highlights her challenge to the conventions of Japanese erotic poetry. She has become a major cult figure for the young in Japan. In the nightclub district of Tokyo, she's known as "Shinjuku's Queen of Poets."

Shusha

Born into a distinguished traditional family in Persia, Shusha grew up in an atmosphere of poetry and mystical chants. Trained as a singer, she learnt the French Chanson and enjoyed a Bohemian student period in Paris. She has written two delightful volumes of memories and had many recordings of her sonorous singing and guitar-playing released. Her voice is much loved for its purity of tone and intensity of emotion, and one of her many talents is a perfect pitch and sensitivity for settings and musical delivery of poems. Her latest CD, *Refugee*, projects a compelling concern for the contemporary victims of political repression. (Photo: Caroline Forbs)

Ifigenija Simonovic

Born in Slovenia, Ifigenija studied Comparative Literature and Slavonic
Linguistics before editing the literary pages of various student
newspapers and youth magazines. She came to Britain in 1978 and now
teaches pottery at Epping Forest College. She also makes her own
exquisite artists' pottery and has Stall 18 at Covent Garden every
Saturday from 10 to 7. She has had her poetry published since she was
thirteen, but in English her only publications have been in New
Departures, *Grandchildren of Albion*, and *Grandchildren of Albion
Live on Cassette* (ND23).

Patti Smith

In 1975 Patti Smith's album *Horses* and her poetry and performances
around New York in the late 1970s almost single-handedly reinvented
the underground rock scene. Four years later, she withdrew from
the public spotlight soon after her major hit, *Because the Night*, written
with Bruce Springsteen. Apart from the release of *Dream of Life* in
1988, she has maintained her self-imposed exile in Detroit, but she has
a new album, *Gone Again*, set for realease in July, and will be touring
Europe extensively, taking in an early set on the Hip Mass. Her prose
poem for Robert Mapplethorpe, *The Coral Sea*, is just out from
Norton & Co. (Photo: Annie Leibovitz)

E J Thribb

Eric Jarvis Thribb, still only 17 1/2, has communicated via Keith's Mum
that he has a lot of time for poetry readings by poets who are good at
reading. He feels that most poets are useless at reading, and he himself
has hardly ever done it aloud, even in private. Nevertheless, he keeps a
private eye on public poetry, and he does think most of the poets
performing at the Poetry Olympics Weekend are OK. He also approves
of the Godfather of the Poetry Olympics, Mike Horovitz, whose latest
book, *Wordsounds & Sightlines*, includes a ten-page 'Fanfare for
Thribb', which closes with the prediction that EJ will ". . . eventually
appear/ Alongside Longfellow,/ Blake and Big Ted/ (To the amazement/
Of Keith's kids)/ In that most golden/ Of treasuries,/ the obituary
column/ Overseen by St Peter/ For the transcen-/ Dentally Private/ Eyes
of eternity." Naturally, Eric is quite chuffed by this tribute. He hopes
that somebody equally gear will have come up by the time he does die to
be able to write a halfway decent elegy for him when that mortal
moment arrives.

Having never given a public reading, EJ anticipates having a certain
amount of stage fright at the Royal Albert Hall. So he is coming with a

friend whom he is confident will be able to read in his place, should the stage fright persist. Keith's Mum is surprised at Eric's interest in the event, because EJ is generally opposed to arty-farty culture-vulture things. But she does agree with him that this whole series looks a bit special. Ray Davies, Nerys Hughes, Christopher Logue, Roger McGough and John Hegley are performers he never dreamed of sharing a bill with. Some of the Private Eye hacks have tried to take the michael out of Horovitz's glorified retirement party, but EJ suspects it may be a case of what he noted in his poem, *In Memoriam Frankie Howerd*: "'Titter ye/ Not.'/ That was/ Frankie Howerd's/ Catchphrase./ No, we shall/ Not titter on/ This solemn Occasion."

Stan Tracey

Stan Tracey's career spans more than five decades of constantly flourishing creativity. He worked with and arranged for many top big bands in the 1950s and was house pianist at Ronnie Scott's first club from 1961 to 1967, playing with most of the modern jazz giants of that era. As composer, bandleader and pianist, he's probably, as Miles Kington thinks, the most original British jazz musician: "His harmonies are satisfyingly crunchy, not marshmallowy; his melody lines have all the quirky rightness of a Goon Show plot; but above all it's his rhythmic approach that gets me in the vitals. Not an extra note is used, not a useless frill, until his routine is as polished as that of one of those breathtaking six-year-old Romanian gymnasts – except that he's actually inventing it on the spot! But why analyse? I could, simply, just sit and listen for hours." Stan's New Quartet is completed by rising star Gerard Presencer on trumpet, his son Clark Tracey on drums, and Andrew Cleyndert on drums. Their first recording, *For Heaven's Sake*, is just out on Cadillac (CAD CD 04).

UNDER MILK WOOD.

Tracey

Evelyn Tubb

Over the last 18 years Evelyn has become a major name in the happy army of musicians and singers seeking out some of the lost treasures of an earlier time. She has made six solo CDs, and her soprano, which will be heard in the SuperJam singing Shakespeare songs with The Broadside Band, was described by the *Musical Times* as ". . . a voice of extraordinary sensitivity in both nuance and colour. Her mimetic and terpsichorean gifts are equally remarkable." She is also much in demand as a teacher, worldwide. (Photo: Sophie Spencer Wood)

Andrei Voznesensky

It's 15 years since Voznesensky was last in Britain, during which years his work and life have gone through many changes. What has remained constant is the brilliance and militantly human commitments of his writing. The most recent volume to appear here was *On the Edge: Poems and Essays from Russia* (translated by Richard McKane, Weidenfeld 1991). Since then, Andrei has worked in Gorbachev's administration on cultural affairs, which he utilised – among other things – to make an enormous exhibition of the paintings of Chagall, which had been locked in vaults for many years. His own work has become closely involved with visual art, developing the genre of the 'video-poem', examples of which will be projected during *A Hip Mass*. Isaiah Berlin has observed how Andrei "is one of the most distinguished, admired and widely read of living Russian poets. Boris Pasternak spoke very highly of his achievement in my presence." Voznesensky is now the President of the Russian P E N Centre.

Keith Waithe & The Macusi Players

Born in Guyana, Waithe has been one of the best kept secrets on the British jazz scene. Together with his Macusi Players, his music represents the cultural diversity and eclectic intermingling of the Caribbean region itself – a fusion of jazz, African, Caribbean and Indian music in a tight matrix of polyrhythmic currents. He himself is not called "the poet of the flute" for nothing – as witness his accompaniment to Grace Nichols on the *Grandchildren of Albion Live* cassette and CD (ND23/24). The group sound of Macusi has just been released on its debut CD, *Magic of Olmec* (Keda Records). The Players are named after the Macusis AmerIndian tribe based in the Savannah region of Guyana, and their music symbolises the gentle, friendly and aesthetic character of this tribe, emphasising the cultural synthesis at its heart. Apart from Keith's vocal and flute effects, the band is comprised of Robert Mitchell on keyboards, Aref Durvesh on tabla, Eustace Williams on electric and double bass, and Cheryl Alleyne on percussion. (Photo: Tim Merry)

Norma Waterson

The Watersons were far and away the most influential harmony
vocal group on the English folk scene in the 1960s. Norma has one of
the strongest and truest voices that this country has ever produced.
She's the third member of Waterson : Carthy, with Martin and their
daughter Eliza.

Heathcote Williams

Heathcote Williams is the author of several award-winning plays,
and a farouche, imaginative actor (Prospero in Jarman's *The Tempest*,
Dr Haggage in *Little Dorritt*). His series of ecological epics, *Whale
Nation*, *Falling for a Dolphin* and *Sacred Elephant* (all Cape) helped the
green movement in very practical ways, alerting many readers to the
way each of these creatures is under terminal threat; they also forged a
deeply moving new style of picture-book. According to the *LRB*,
"He's a creature of extremes; possessed of a remarkable intellect, gentle
and generous in life, he can rise in his plays to heights of piercing
illumination." He's a talented poet, juggler, fire-eater, painter, wood-
carver and conjuror. His high energy performance at a previous Poetry
Olympics was likened by Alan Brien to "Alexander Pope on speed."

Jah Wobble

After emerging as a key member of Public Image Ltd (PIL), Jah Wobble
threw himself into a bewildering and myriad range of projects
that found him light years ahead of his contemporaries in exploring
new and interesting sounds, and a critics' favourite. In a career that
has now spanned seventeen years, Wobble has always managed
to surprise, confound and delight his core audience. His latest album,
The Inspiration of William Blake, will be released by All Saints/
30 Hertz in September.

Kit Wright

Kit Wright was born in Kent in 1944, and educated at Berkhampsted School and New College, Oxford. He taught in a South London comprehensive and then spent three years lecturing in English Literature at Brock University, Ontario. He was Education Secretary to the Poetry Society and Commoner in the Creative Arts at Trinity College, Cambridge. He has published twelve volumes of poetry, nine of them for children, all very popular. His poetry has been acclaimed by the *TLS* for its "great variety, real accomplishment and most important, sheer enjoyability." Many of his poems have been heard on radio and television and he frequently gives entertaining and lively poetry readings. He also teaches regularly in workshops for both adults and children.

Zila

It means "We are Here" in Xhosa. The group was formed by the late Dudu Pukwana, to celebrate the native music of South Africa. They remain an exciting multi-national band, playing a rich mix of township jazz, soul, gospel and funk. Their performances are exuberant, sophisticated and stylish, full of passion and soul, melody and power. The Zila musicians playing with Progress on SuperJam are Mervyn Africa (piano), Lucky Ranku (guitar), Ollie Crook (bass) and Shawn Stephenson (drums).

Acknowledgements

John Agard: 'Utterance', *Lovelines for a Goat-Bom Lady* (Serpent's Tail, 1990)

Patience Agbabi, 'Accidentally Falling', R.A.W. (Gecko Press, 1995)

Damon Albarn: Three lyrics, Parklife (Parlophone/EMI 1994)

James Berry: 'On an Afternoon train from Purley to Victoria, 1955', *Hot Earth Cold Earth* (Bloodaxe 1995)

Sujata Bhatt: 'Chutney' *The Stinking Rose* (Carcanet, 1995)

Valerie Bloom: 'Sun a-shine, rain a-fall, Rain a-fall', *Duppy Jamboree and other Jamaican Poems* (CUP, 1992)

Nina Cassian: 'Language', 'Description of the Hand' *Cheerleader for a Funeral* (Forest Books, 1992); 'A Famous Woman', 'Repetitio' *Life Sentence: Selected Poems* (Anvil Press Poetry, 1990)

Carol Ann Duffy: 'Litany' *Selected Poems* (Penguin Books in association with Anvil Press Poetry, 1994)

Paul Durcan: 'Raymond of the Rooftops' *The Berlin Wall Cafe* (Harvill, 1995)

James Fenton: 'The Mistake' *Out of Danger* (Penguin, 1993)

Miroslav Holub: 'Great Ancestors' *Vanishing Lung Syndrome* (Fabers 1990)

Jackie Kay: 'Dance of the Cherry Blossoms' *The Adoption Papers* (Bloodaxe, 1991)

Gwyneth Lewis: 'The Telegraph Baby' *Parables & Faxes* (Bloodaxe 1995)

Adrian Mitchell: 'A Puppy Called Puberty' *Blue Coffee* (Bloodaxe 1996)

Grace Nichols: 'Sugar Cane' *The Fat Black Woman's Poems* (Virago 1984)

Ben Okri: 'On a Picture of a South African Street' *An African Elegy* (Cape 1992)

Kazuko Shiraishi: 'Yellow Lake', 'Woodpecker' *Burning Meditations and Other Poems* Pink Sand Studio, Japan, 1991; 'Little Planet' *Little Planet and other poems* (Shichigatsudo, Tokyo, 1994)

Patti Smith: 'Burning Roses' *Early Work*, (Plexus, 1994); 'Farewell Reel' *Patti Smith Gone Again* (Arista/BMG Records 1996)

EJ Thribb: 'In Memoriam: Dizzy Gillespie and Rudolph Nureyev', 'In Memoriam: Timothy Leary LSD' *Private Eye* magazine 1993, 1995

Andrei Voznesensky: 'The prisoners make the seat-covers for Aeroflot' *On the Edge: Poems and Essays from Russia* (Weidenfeld & Nicholson, 1991); 'Wiper' dice book (Moscow 1994)

Kit Wright: 'I Found South African Breweries Most Hospitable' *Poems 1974–1983* (Hutchinson 1988); 'Rock Around the Wok' *Great Snakes!* (Penguin Children's Books, 1994)

W

The Waterstone's
Guide to Poetry Books
is being published on
National Poetry Day

Thursday 10th October 1996

Call Nick Rennison on 0181 996 4330 for more details.

books to celebrate poetry

GRANDCHILDREN OF ALBION: VOICES AND VISIONS OF YOUNGER POETS IN BRITAIN

Michael Horovitz (ed)

New Departures/Airlift £9.99

This lavishly illustrated 400-page anthology is the revival issue of New Departures (numbers 17--20), and has been described in the London Evening Standard as "crackling with more energy than the national grid", and in Time Out as "exemplary in its endorsement of multiracial work . . . the essential buy for poetry lovers."

There are substantial selections from 40 poets, most of whom come to their most essential life giving readings, and/or projecting their texts in collaboration with various forms of music. They also relish connecting with each other and with every kind of audience, in multiple permutations, on the Live New Departures/Poetry Olympics bandwagons. Writers from the book most readily available, singly or in groups, to give performances, talks, readings or jam sessions, include: --

Fiona Pitt-Kethley

Ifigenija Zagoricnik

Linton Kwesi Johnson

Sujata Bhatt

Grace Nichols

Michèle Roberts

Carol Ann Duffy

Neil Sparkes

Adam Horovitz,

Jean Binta Bréeze

Mahmood Jamal

Donal Carroll

These are the twelve poets featured on the first Grandchildren of Albion LIVE ON CASSETTE and (excepting Adam Horovitz & Ifigenija Zagoricnik) on the first GofA LIVE ON CD recordings - with music by Keith Waithe on the Caribbean flute & Dick Heckstall-Smith on tenor & soprano saxophones, both of whom, along with jazz-poetry by composer-pianist Stan Tracey & grandfather/editor Michael Horovitz, are also available for gigs of all kinds.

Michael Horovitz

Keith Waithe/

Dick Heckstall-Smith

Order Form To:

New Departures, PO Box 9819, London W11 2GQ

Name..

Address..

....

....

Please send

(enter number of copies wanted in bracket (s) of your choice): –

(   ) **Grandchildren of Albion Live on Cassette** Volume One
      (95 minutes –*NDC 23*) at £8 each including VAT
      plus 75p towards post and packing

(   ) **Grandchildren of Albion Live on CD** Volume One
      (78 minutes –*NDCD 24*) at £10.50 each including VAT
      plus £1 post and packing
      *(CD differs from cassette in that all Ifigenija Zagoricnik-Simonovic's and
      Adam Horovitz's sets are omitted, as are Donal Carroll's second and third poems.)*

(   ) **Grandchildren of Albion Anthology**
      (400-page illustrated –*ND17-20*) at £9.99
      plus £1.50 post & packing

(   ) **Michael Horovitz's rural Midsummer Morning Jog Log,**
      (Paperback edition) illustrated by Peter Blake, at £3.50
      plus 75p for post and packing

(   ) **Midsummer Morning Jog Log** rhapsody,
      (Clothbound edition) illustrated by Peter Blake, at £8.95
      plus £1 for post and packing

(   ) **Wordsounds and Sightlines: New and Selected Poems**
      by Michael Horovitz
      at £6.99 plus 75p for post and packing

I enclose a crossed cheque/postal order for £   to cover the total cost of this order including postage and packing, made out to *New Departures*, to the PO Box address.

NB. If ordering outside the UK please *double* the amount for post and packing. Allow 21 days for delivery (or longer for outside the UK).

For more information about the contents of any of these titles; back issues of *New Departures*, and of Michael & Frances Horovitz's books – including (multi-) signed editions available; and/or of readings and events to come, please enclose extra postage and indicate particular interests.

Autographs

Special thanks to —

Air Lingus
Donatella Bernstein
Peter Boizot
Fiona Campbell
The British Council
Dennis Publishing
Juliet Eve
Polly & Andy Garnett
Robert Gutterman
John Hampson
Hyperactive Ltd
Judith Keyston
Ashley Knowles
Linda McCartney
Helen Maleed
Gillian Marcelle
Richard Mellor
the Poetry Society
Private Eye
David Russell
the Science Photo Library
Ruth Vaughn
Shelley Warren

and
hundreds of others